Pitman Po
of Busines

Pitman Pocket Dictionary of Business Terms

John Old • Tony Shafto •
with Shu Lun Wong

Pitman

PITMAN PUBLISHING LIMITED
128 Long Acre, London WC2E 9AN

A Longman Group Company

© John Old, Tony Shafto and Shu Lun Wong 1986

First published in Great Britain 1986

British Library Cataloguing in Publication Data

Old, John
  Pitman pocket dictionary of business terms.
  1. Business—Dictionaries
  I. Title II. Shafto, T.A.C. III. Wong, Shu Lun
  338.6′03′21   HF1001

ISBN 0-273-02412-4

All rights reserved. No part of this publication may be reproduced, stored in a retrieval system, or transmitted, in any form or by any means, electronic, mechanical, photocopying, recording and/or otherwise, without the prior written permission of the publishers. This book may not be lent, resold, hired out or otherwise disposed of by way of trade in any form of binding or cover other than that in which it is published, without the prior consent of the publishers. This book is sold subject to the Standard Conditions of Sale of Net Books and may not be resold in the UK below the net price.

Printed and bound in Great Britain by
Richard Clay (The Chaucer Press) Ltd,
Bungay, Suffolk

Preface

This dictionary contains over 3000 entries, providing a comprehensive coverage of all aspects of business and commerce.

It is thoroughly up-to-date and international in flavour, making it ideal for all those beginning a business career, for all students of business subjects and as a handy reference book for business people.

The selection of entries reflects both common and specialized use of terms as well as changes in usage in recent years. Frequently used abbreviations and acronyms are included. Copious cross-referencing guides the user easily through related terms.

John Old has spent many years as a business and economics lecturer after studying at the London School of Economics and Warwick University.

Tony Shafto is an Oxford graduate and has worked extensively in industry and education and is the successful author of several business studies textbooks.

Shu Lun Wong, born in China, graduated from Durham University Business School, has worked in industry and education in Hong Kong, Ghana, the USA, the United Kingdom and Canada.

A

A1 First class, derived from the ship classification A1 at Lloyd's.

abatement This has the general meaning of reduction and is found in connection with such terms as abatement of a legacy, of a nuisance, of rent but is also used to refer to stopping a legal action that has already commenced.

above par Higher than the nominal value, used of shares and other financial securities.

above the line Taken into account in calculating gross profit.

absenteeism Non-attendance of workers for scheduled work.

absorption costing Costing that takes into account all costs associated with production, including fixed and variable costs.

a/c Account. See *account*

A/C Account current. A statement setting out in debit and credit form an account of the transactions between two parties during an agreed trading period.

ACAS (Advisory, Conciliation and Arbitration Service) A British state-financed but independent body which assists in resolving labour disputes and generally seeks to improve employer-employee relations.

accelerated depreciation The writing down of an asset's value in the firm's accounts at a faster rate.

acceleration clause A condition in an agreement to the effect that, if repayments fall into arrears, the whole amount becomes due.

accept a bill Agree to make a payment as set out in a bill of exchange by writing one's name across its face.

acceptance The act of accepting a bill. Also used to refer to an accepted bill.

acceptance for honour The acceptance of a bill not yet due for payment by someone not already a party to it to provide security or additional security to satisfy the bill's holder and preserve the good name of the person liable to make the payment.

acceptance sampling A technique in quality control based on taking a sample from a process to check that an acceptable quality has been obtained.

acceptance supra protest The acceptance of a bill by another party after it has been *protested*.

acceptilation A Scottish term for a formal discharge or release from a debt.

accepting house A merchant bank which accepts and, therefore, guarantees payment of a bill on behalf of approved customers. Such bills are known as *bank bills*.

acceptor The person who has agreed to make the payment stipulated by a bill of exchange and who has signed across its face.

access time In computing, the time taken to retrieve information from a *storage location*. The information may be a computer program or a set of data.

accident book A record of industrial accidents that firms in the UK are required, by law, to maintain.

accident, industrial An incident in the course of work resulting in personal injury.

accommodation bill A bill of exchange to which a person lends his or her name to oblige another and thereby provides a guarantee of payment.

account 1. Regular customer of a firm, especially in advertising. 2. A categorized list of financial transactions. 3. A continuing credit arrangement between a firm and its customers (also *charge account*). 4. A trading period for organized markets employing a clearing system for payments, especially stock exchanges. 5. A statement showing the amount due by one person to another for cash, goods, etc.

account day Day established in a stock exchange for the settlement of bargains entered into by members. They are usually at roughly fortnightly intervals. In the London exchange they are normally the second Monday after the close of each account.

account executive Member of an advertising agency responsible for dealings with a particular client.

account payable Money owed by a firm for goods and services bought but not yet paid for. US term equivalent to UK *creditor*.

account receivable Money owed to a firm for goods and services bought but not yet paid for. US term equivalent to UK *debtor*.

account rendered Account submitted to a customer for moneys due for goods and services, details of which are sent separately.

account sales An account sent by a merchant to the consignor of goods, or by a broker to his principal, showing details of goods sold, prices obtained and the net amount payable after deducting all approved expenses.

account stated An agreed account of transactions between sellers and buyers.

accountancy The profession concerned with the making up and analysis of accounts and with related matters of financial management and negotiation.

accountant One who is a member of the accountancy profession and is concerned with the making up and/or the analysis of accounts and with their use by organizations.

accounting period Period covered by the accounts of a firm between the drawing up of balance sheets. Equivalent to US *fiscal period*.

accrual An *accrued expense* is one that is incurred over a period of time but which becomes payable on a fixed date. For example, if rent is payable quarterly in March, the accrued expense in January is one-third of the amount due in March. Similarly an *accrued revenue* represents a debt accumulating and payable to one at a date in the future.

acid test ratio A measure of a firm's liquidity and hence its ability to meet its short-term financial commitments, based on the division of current assets, other than stocks, by current liabilities. Also known as *quick ratio*.

acquisition purchase of one firm by another.

acquittance A full discharge in writing of some contract, debt or liability.

act of bankruptcy Any act by which a debtor becomes liable to be made a bankrupt, for example an act designed to defraud creditors.

act of God Any sudden or violent act of nature, such as an earthquake, which could not have been prevented by human intervention or forethought.

action Any civil proceedings instituted in a court of law.

active bonds Bonds which bear a fixed rate of interest payable in full from the date of issue.

active circulation The active circulation of a bank of issue means the notes actually issued and in the hands of the public.

active partner One who takes a working part in the business of which he is part owner.

activity chart A chart used to describe the breakdown of the structure of a department by specifying what each person does. It provides the *systems analyst* with an indication of the worker-hours involved in the workload of the department.

activity ratio Financial ratio relating sales revenue to a particular class of assets.

activity sampling A management control system which involves observations of workers' activities at randomly selected times.

actuary One who applies mathematical and statistical science to studies of mortality, life expectation and related matters, including the calculation of insurance, pension, annuity and other rates dependent on these.

ad extremum To the extreme.

ad infinitum To infinity.

ad interim In the meanwhile.

ad libitum At pleasure.

ad referendum Subject to further consideration.

ad valorem According to value.

address In computing, the name or number used to locate a particular item of information in the computer memory.

adjudication order An order made by the Court of Bankruptcy declaring a debtor bankrupt so that his or her estate may be placed in the hands of a trustee and wound up for the benefit of creditors.

adjusting entry Entry made in accounts, not to show a new transaction, but to record earlier entries more accurately, e.g. by correcting errors or re-designating expenses.

adjustment An insurance term for the settlement of a claim made under an insurance policy.

administration expense The expense of formulating, directing and controlling the policy, organization and operation of a business.

administration order An order made by the Court, in cases of small bankruptcies, for the summary administration of a debtor's estate.

administrator 1. A person appointed by the law for the purpose of winding up the estate of a dead person where there is no effective executor for a will or no will at all. 2. A person appointed to administer the affairs of an insolvent company under the provisions of insolvency legislation introduced in 1985.

ADP Automatic data processing. See *data processing*.

ADR Accord dangereux routiers. European

agreement concerning the carriage of dangerous goods by road.

advance A prepayment, especially one made at the commencement of a transaction on account of the full amount due to be paid later.

advance corporation tax In UK company taxation the tax deducted at source from shareholders' dividends and which can then be offset against a firm's liability to corporation tax.

advance freight Freight charges paid before shipment.

advanced text management This component of *electronic office* facilities includes proof reading, fitting text to a required line length and language translation.

advice The action by a home bank, the *advising bank* of sending the documents required under an unconfirmed *documentary letter of credit* to a foreign *issuing bank* for collection and payment.

advice note A letter informing the receiver that a transaction, especially the consignment of goods, has been or is about to be effected.

advocate 1. One who speaks on behalf of another. 2. (especially USA and Scotland) One who represents and pleads the case of another in a court of law. 3. One who speaks in support of a cause or proposal.

affidavit A declaration made in writing, upon oath, before a person empowered to administer an oath.

affiliate 1. A closely connected or associated person or body, e.g. the subsidiary of a firm or a member union of the TUC. 2. (USA) An affiliated company is the American equivalent of the British *associated company*.

AFL-CIO American Federation of Labor-Congress of Industrial Organizations.

after date Term used in connection with certain bills of exchange when these are made payable a stated period after the date of the bill.

after sales service Maintenance and repair facilities made available to customers after the sale and delivery of goods.

after sight Term used in connection with bills of exchange when these are made payable a stated period after the date of acceptance of the bill.

agate line (USA) A measure of advertising space in newspapers.

age admitted An endorsement to an insurance policy indicating that the insurer is satisfied with proof of the life assured's age and will not require further evidence of this at the time of claim.

agency shop A working establishment in which a trade union is recognized for negotiations on behalf of all workers, whether members of that union or not, at that establishment. Workers are expected to pay subscriptions to the union but need not join it.

agenda A list of business to be done in the order that

agent One who is authorized to represent and make legally binding agreements on behalf of a principal or one who buys or sells on behalf of another.

AGM Annual general meeting. 1. The statutory yearly meeting of shareholders of a company. 2. The principal meeting held once a year to which all members of a formally constituted group are invited. The principal purposes of an AGM are that the past year's officers should account to the members for their activities and conduct during the year and to make any necessary elections for the next year's officers

AI Artificial intelligence.

air waybill A waybill used for airfreight. See also *consignment note*.

ALGOL (from algorithmic language) A computer programming language with particularly useful mathematical applications.

algorithm A prescribed set of well-defined rules giving a sequence of operations for the solution of a problem.

alienation 1. The conveyance of property to others. 2. An attitude of hostility on the part of workers towards their employers or towards their work.

allonge A slip attached to a bill of exchange to

contain further endorsements when there is no further space on the bill itself.

allotment letter Letter sent to applicants for new shares informing them of the quantity of shares allocated to them in response to the application.

all-round price A price which includes all items normally charged as extras over the basic price.

AMA American Management Association.

amalgamation The process whereby two or more organizations join together to form one. See also *merger*.

amortisation or amortisement 1. (finance) The redemption of loans or bonds by annual payments from a *sinking fund*. 2. (law) The *alienation* of lands by way of transfer in perpetuity to a corporation or charity. 3. (accounting) The provision for the using up of a wasting asset, e.g. oil fields, mines or quarries.

AMT Air mail transfer. A method of transferring money in foreign trade.

analog (analogue) computer A computer which operates with physical data represented by measurable physical quantities, e.g. the length or strength of an electrical impulse. Contrast *digital computer*.

annual report In the UK this is the yearly report required by law to be made by the directors of a company.

annual return In the UK, details of a company's affairs and in particular, the summarized accounts that must, by law, be filed with the Registrar of Companies.

annuity A sum of money received every year for an agreed number of years or during the lifetime of the payee – the *annuitant*.

ante-date To date any letter or document before the true date.

antitrust (especially USA) Pertaining to laws or other government activity to suppress monopolistic abuses and encourage competition.

a/o Account of.

application In computing, the task of group of tasks for which the computer is being used.

application software A program or group of associated programs directed at some generic application.

appraisement or appraisal Valuation of property or a project.

appreciation A rise in value, particularly of currencies.

apprentice One who enters into a contract to work for an employer for an agreed period in return for training in certain skills.

appropriated goods Goods surplus at the completion of a vessel's discharge and delivered by the shipowner in place of goods short-delivered.

appropriation account An account showing the use of funds generated in a trading period. Equivalent to US *retained income statement*.

APR Annual percentage rate. The true annual rate of interest, taking into account such factors as the periodic repayments of the principal and payments of interest at intervals of less than a year.

arbitrage The purchase of currency or financial securities in one market for re-sale in another, usually in another country, in anticipation of profit.

arbitration The resolution of a dispute by an independent person or persons, the *arbitrator(s)*, acceptable to all parties to the dispute.

arbitration of exchange Calculating the proportional rates of currency exchange between various countries to see if it is more advantageous to make a payment directly in another country in that country's currency or to make it indirectly by way of one or more other countries.

Ariel A computerized system for dealing in shares on the British Stock Exchange, used chiefly by insurance offices.

arrears Amounts remaining unpaid after the time due for repayment has expired.

arrestment Scottish law equivalent of English *attachment*.

articles of association In a joint stock company, the

document specifying the rules and conditions governing the internal affairs of the company.

articles of partnership The formal, written statement of the rights and obligations that the members of a partnership have agreed to hold between themselves.

a/s 1. Account sales. 2. After sight. See *bill of exchange*. 3. Alongside (a ship).

assay Chemically testing and analysing pieces of metal, minerals, etc., to determine their purity and ascertain the percentage of foreign matter.

ASCII American standard code for information interchange. A widely used standard character computer encoding scheme.

assembly line A system of production in which work in progress is moved from place to place where successive operations are carried out, the whole process of production being subdivided into separate, routine activities.

asset stripping The purchase of a firm which is still in productive operation for less than the total value of its assets with the objective of ceasing operations and selling the assets at a profit or converting them to more profitable uses.

assets The goods and property of all kinds belonging to an organization or person and which are available to meet debts or liabilities.

assign To make a legal transfer of property or documents of title to property to another, the *assignee*.

assignment 1. A transfer of any personal property or right to another. 2. The document whereby such a transfer is made.

assisted area or region An area or region in the UK which is entitled to receive regional development assistance from either the British Government or the European Communities.

associated company A company in which another has a shareholding sufficient to allow it to have a significant influence on policy matters.

assurance Equivalent to *insurance* but used most frequently in relation to life insurance business.

at and from A marine insurance term which covers insurance while the vessel is at a specified port as well as on a voyage therefrom.

at best An instruction to a stockbroker to sell shares or stock at the best available price, whatever that might be.

at call The terms of a deposit with a financial institution. The deposit is repayable on demand without notice.

at par The situation when the market value and the nominal, face or official value are the same. The term is applied to stocks and shares and to currency with a fixed exchange rate.

at sight A term used on bills of exchange which are payable on demand.

ATA A combination of *Admission Temporaire* and

Temporary Admission. A widely used *carnet* permitting the temporary import of business samples and goods used for demonstration and exhibition.

ATP Accord transports périssables. A European agreement concerning the international carriage of perishable foodstuffs by road and the conditions that should be met by vehicles used to convey such foodstuffs. Hence *ATP certificate* – a certificate of compliance with the required conditions.

ATR Admission temporaire roulette. Temporary admission on wheels. A *carnet* allowing the temporary admission of wheeled vehicles such as caravans.

attachment 1. Laying an embargo upon, prohibiting the sale or disposal of a debtor's money or goods in the hands of third parties, pending the settlement of some claim against the owner. 2. Compulsory deduction from earnings as a result of a Court order.

attested copy True or verified copy of an original document – not a copy of a copy – and examined or collated by two persons and certified as a true copy by a declaration to that effect signed by them and written on the copy.

attorney 1. One legally qualified to practise in a court of law. 2. One authorized by a *power of attorney* to act on behalf of another. See *power of attorney*.

auction A method of selling property by competition. The most general method is for a professional *auctioneer* to offer the property for sale to persons assembled by advertisement, who compete for the purchase by bids or offers of sums of money. The person who bids last, or who bids the highest amount, is declared the purchaser provided the bid is up to any *reserve price* previously declared to the auctioneer by the seller.

In a *Dutch Auction* the auctioneer commences by naming a high price and gradually reduces it until someone closes with the offer.

audit A searching examination of all books, accounts, original sales and purchase documents, etc., by one termed an *auditor* who, in the case of a limited company in the UK, must be a member of a professional body approved by statute and appointed with the authority of shareholders.

authorized capital The capital of a company as authorized in its memorandum of association. Also known as *nominal* and *registered* capital.

Autocode A low level computer language.

av Average.

a/v Ad valorem. According to value.

aval An endorsement on a bill of exchange or promissory note by someone other than the drawer. The endorsement provides a guarantee of payment.

AVCO From *average cost*, a system of valuing stock changes. The average unit cost of stock is multiplied by the amount of stock at the end of the time period.

average 1. A figure used to typify a set of data, found by one of the following: *mode*, the most common item; *median*, the value of the central item in a ranked series; (most frequently) the *arithmetic mean*, the series total divided by the number of items it contains. 2. An insurance term which refers to a method of calculating a loss. In marine assurance *particular average* relates to damage to or loss of specific cargo while *general average* relates to a loss sustained to save the rest of the cargo and which is shared by all owners. In fire insurance, average relates to the position when property is insured for less than full value and a policy 'subject to average' provides compensation only for that proportion of the loss that the sum insured bears to the actual value, the insured person being regarded as the insurer for the difference.

average adjuster A professional person appointed by insurers to negotiate settlement of an insurance claim. Also known as a *loss adjuster*.

averaging A system whereby a speculator increases his transactions at a higher or lower figure when the price is unfavourable so that a smaller proportionate favourable movement in price will cancel out the loss. For example, if a share price fell 100p or $10 the holder of 1000 shares might purchase a further 1000 so that a rise of only 50p or $5 would average out the loss and profit.

AWB *Air waybill*.

B

BAA British Airports Authority.

back An abbreviation of *backwardation*.

back-bond A bond given in return for a loan by the absolute owner of property reducing his right to that property to that of trustee. The full ownership right is recoverable on repayment of the loan.

backdate To provide for a payment, wage settlement, document, etc., to apply from a date in the past.

back-freight The additional freight chargeable on the return of goods not accepted at the port of delivery.

backing store The computer memory or storage system within which information is stored for reference rather than for direct execution.

back-to-back credits A merchant who has purchased and re-sold goods and who has had a *documentary credit* opened in his favour by the buyer may be able to arrange for a bank to open a second credit on the security of the first, in favour of the seller. The two documentary credits are known as 'back-to-back credits' and they must concern the same consignment of goods. The arrangement is suitable for such cases as a UK merchant acting as intermediary for a sale between two other countries, e.g. to provide the additional security of a UK merchant and bank or to keep the identity of the original seller hidden from the ultimate buyer who may prefer to remain officially ignorant of the real source for, say, political reasons.

back-up A copy of computer programs taken for reasons of safety and normally stored separately from the original.

backwardation 1. (UK stock exchange) A charge made on the seller of stock by its buyer when the former carries the bargain forward into the next account. 2. (commodity exchanges) Amount by which the *spot* price exceeds the *forward* price.

bad debt A debt that is likely never to be paid.

bailee One to whom goods are delivered in trust upon a contract.

bailiff 1. An officer of the Court responsible for enforcing its judgements, in particular by seizing property in payment of debts. 2. An agent or land-steward.

bailment Delivery of goods by one person, the *bailor* to another, the *bailee*, in trust, upon the understanding that they are returned when the purpose for which they were bailed has been fulfilled.

balance In accounting, the difference between the totals of the debit and credit entries in an account.

balance of payments A summary of the payments into and out of a country in a given time period.

The *current balance* includes all payments for goods, including capital goods (the *balance of visibles*) and for services and for some transfers of income and revenue (the *balance of invisibles*). The final balance also includes capital, mostly investment, transactions and 'official financing' payments such as government borrowings and repayments.

balance of trade A description usually applied to the *balance of visibles*, the summary of imports and exports of goods into and out of a country in a given time period. Sometimes it is used in the sense of the *current balance of payments*.

balance receipt A document issued to a transferor of shares whose share certificate is for a larger number of shares than is being transferred.

balance sheet A statement showing the assets and liabilities of an organization at a stated date, especially the last date of the organization's financial year.

balance ticket See *balance receipt*.

balloon note A loan repayable in a series of small amounts and a large final payment.

Baltic Exchange The Baltic Mercantile and Shipping Exchange. 1. Commodity market specializing in grain, coal, oil seeds and timber. 2. The world's largest market for shipping and aircraft services.

bank A firm specializing in the holding of deposits, lending money, acting as a monetary agent and advisor on behalf of customers and providing money transmission facilities such as cheques and credit transfer. In the UK the term 'bank' is reserved by law for institutions approved and licensed by the Bank of England.

bank bill 1. A bill of exchange issued or accepted by a bank. Such a bill, carrying in effect the guarantee of a well known bank, is more widely negotiable and can be discounted at more favourable rates than other bills. Terms of payment frequently specify 'payment by bank bill'. 2. (USA) A bank note.

bank card A term often used to refer to a *cheque guarantee card*. See *cheque guarantee card*.

bank holiday (UK) A day stipulated by Parliament as a day on which the banks are to be closed for business with the implication that most other business organizations will also close and their employees enjoy a holiday.

bank lodgement form A checklist of instructions prepared by an exporter on a form supplied by and returned to a bank, to ensure that the bank has clear and full instructions concerning the exporter's requirements under a *documentary letter of credit*.

bank note Printed paper money, usually issued by or under the authority of a country's central bank, in the UK the Bank of England. In the UK, notes in circulation have denominations of £1, £5, £10, £20 and £50. In 1984 the £1 note began to be replaced by the £1 coin. Bank of England notes and the £1 coin are *unlimited legal tender*.

Bank of England The central bank of the United Kingdom. It is publicly owned and acts as the government's bank. In addition it administers the government's monetary policy, licenses banks and licensed deposit takers, issues bank notes and coin and acts as lender of last resort to the banking system.

bank paper Bills that have been drawn, accepted or endorsed by a bank.

bank rate The term formerly used for the official re-discount, or lending rate, at which the Bank of England is prepared to re-discount bills for the discount houses.

bank returns A weekly statement, issued by the national banks, showing the amount of gold, silver and bullion in hand, the value of bills discounted, the amount of notes and coin in circulation, the value of securities held, and all other particulars necessary to show the banks' financial position.

bank statement Statements issued periodically to bank customers showing details of payments and receipts since the previous statement.

bankers' cheques Cheques drawn by one banker on another, sometimes given to customers as a method of remitting money from one place to another.

Bankers' Clearing House See *clearing*.

bankers' draft A form of cheque drawn by a bank on one of its branches or on another bank, often in another country. Subject to the reputation of the bank they are equivalent to bank notes and useful as a means of conveying or transferring money between countries.

bankers' order A written order given by a bank customer instructing the bank to make a payment or series of payments from an account on stated dates. Also known as a *standing order*.

bankrupt A person declared by the Court and publicly announced to be insolvent and unable to meet his or her debts. The person remains bankrupt until *discharged* by order of the Court.

bankruptcy The condition of being bankrupt.

banks of issue Banks authorized to issue their own notes. The Bank of England has a monopoly of the note issue in England and Wales. Some Scottish banks issue their own notes but each of these must be backed by Bank of England notes.

bar chart An illustration using bars, usually horizontal and indicating the progress of activities listed down the left hand column. It is often used for planning and scheduling and it enables actual performance to be measured against planned or estimated performance. See also *Gantt chart*.

bar code A printed, machine-readable code that consists of parallel bars of varied width and spacing. The codes on household goods are made up of 30 bars to provide a unique 13 digit code number for each product.

bareboat charter A ship hiring contract under which the charterer pays all expenses during the period of hire.

bargain 1. Any transaction in stocks and shares. 2. An agreement for the purchase or sale of anything. 3. The thing bought or sold. 4. Any cheap or advantageous purchase.

bargain and sale A contract under seal, whereby real estate, lands, tenements whether in possession, reversion, or remainder, are conveyed from one person to another for a consideration.

barratry Any malicious or unlawful acts committed by the master or crew of a vessel, whereby its owners are exposed to injury. Among these may be classed the sinking or deserting of a ship, delaying or defeating her voyage, smuggling, running off with a ship, or wilfully carrying her out of her prescribed course; or any offence whereby a ship or her cargo may be subjected to arrest, detention, forfeiture or loss.

barrister An advocate admitted to plead at the bar of the English law courts, corresponding to the title *advocate* in Scotland.

barter The exchanging of one commodity for another without the employment of money or any other medium of exchange.

26 base rate

base rate The rate of interest declared by an individual bank and which forms the basis of interest rates allowed on deposits and charged on loans.

base year The year from which changes in an index, e.g. the Index of Retail Prices, are calculated.

BASIC Beginner's All-purpose Symbolic Instruction Code. A computer programming language commonly used for microcomputers.

batch production The production of goods in small, intermittent runs.

baud rate In computing, the number of times per second that a system, especially a data transmission channel, changes state.

b/d Brought down (in book-keeping).

B/E Bill of exchange.

bear A speculator who sells, for delivery on a certain date, stocks, shares or other securities which he or she does not possess, in the expectation of being able to buy them at a lower price before the delivery date arrives and so make a profit from the transaction. Because a 'bear' is expecting prices to fall the term *bear market* has come to mean a market in which prices are tending to fall.

bearer bond A bond the ownership of which is not recorded by the issuer and which can, therefore, be transferred by the holder simply giving it to another.

bearer cheque See *cheque to bearer*.

bearer scrip A document issued by a government or company in respect of a new issue where only part of the full price has been paid. It is a temporary document and remains in being until all instalments have been paid and the definitive bond issued. It is treated as a negotiable instrument.

bed and breakfasting The sale and repurchase of assets in rapid succession, typically for taxation, balance sheet or liquidity reasons.

Beerbohm's List A daily report giving particulars of the grain trade and markets.

below par Stocks, shares and other securities are said to be below par when their market prices are below their nominal, face value.

below the line Not taken into account in calculating (especially) gross profit.

benchmark 1. The surveyor's mark, usually cut in stone or rock, used to indicate the starting or other significant point in a series of levels used to measure altitudes. 2. A term used generally to indicate a standard by which other features can be measured. 3. In computing, a problem or task designed so that a system can be measured and evaluated for its performance in completing a known workload.

beneficiary One who benefits under a will or trust.

bequest A gift of personal property made by a will.

Better Business Bureau (USA) One of a number of

voluntary organizations that promote consumer interests.

b/f Brought forward.

bid To offer a price, typically in an auction.

bid price The lower price offered by a stock market dealer or unit trust. The price at which the dealer or trust is willing to buy.

big figure A term used in the foreign exchange market for the main digits of an exchange rate. For example for a rate of $1.4038 the $1.40 is the big figure.

big four Term applied to the four large 'High Street' clearing banks in the UK. They are Barclays, National Westminster, Lloyds and Midland.

bill There are a number of different 'bills' but when the term is used on its own it usually refers to a bill of exchange. See *bill of exchange*.

bill books Records of bills receivable (payable to the firm) and payable.

bill of entry Also referred to as an *entry* or *entry form*. The statement of the nature and value of goods made to the Customs authorities. Efforts are continually being made to simplify international trade documentation. The UK authorities require an *import entry* which takes various forms depending on the nature of the goods and the facilities available at the port for processing documents. Computerized import entry procedures are likely to replace older forms of documentation.

bill of exchange An open letter of request addressed by one person (the drawer) to another (the drawee) requesting payment of a definite sum of money from the latter to the former. The bill is said to be *accepted* once signed by the drawee or on his or her behalf, guaranteeing payment. *Sight* bills are payable immediately; *time* bills are payable at some specified future date. A bill payable *to order* is payable to whoever the legal holder is on the payment date. Such bills are *negotiable instruments* and may be sold by the original drawer to another party for some fraction of the full amount payable. This is known as *discounting* the bill. The drawer or subsequent holder *endorses* the bill by signing it by name and passes it to the discounting bank or house for cash. British bills may be *inland*, referring to amounts payable within the UK or *foreign*, referring to amounts arising from international transactions. Bills of exchange, also known as *commercial bills* to distinguish them from *treasury bills* issued by the government, are important sources of short-time finance as many institutions are prepared to advance credit on the security of bills accepted by those banks whose 'paper' is eligible for re-discounting by the Bank of England. Such a bank bill is literally as good as a Bank of England note.

bill of lading (B/L) Although declining as more and more freight is carried by container, roll-on, roll-off and other methods of road transport with simplified document procedures, the bill of lading remains an important document, especially for trade with non-European countries. It has three important elements. These are: 1. evidence of a contract between the exporter or importer and a shipping company for the carriage of goods by sea; 2. a receipt for goods shipped and evidence of their condition when accepted on board ship; 3. a document of title which is also a negotiable instrument, i.e. ownership of the goods can be transferred by transfer of title on the B/L. See also *clean B/L* and *received for shipment B/L*.

bill of material A list of the type and quantities of materials required to make a product.

bill of sale 1. A document transferring ownership but not possession of something to another, often as security for a loan. 2. A form of contract for the transfer of ships or shares in ships.

bill of sight A temporary entry form allowing the landing and Customs examination of goods whose precise descriptions, qualities, etc., are not known to the importer. Under modern simplified procedures inspection or sampling can usually be arranged by written or, if examination only is required, verbal request.

bill rate The discount rate applied by banks and discount houses for bills of exchange.

bills payable Bills of exchange for which the holder is responsible for payment.

bills receivable Bills of exchange to whose payments the holder is entitled.

binary A number system using a base of two. It is well suited for computer use because it can represent the presence or absence of a signal such as an electrical impulse.

bin tag (or card) A tag attached to a bin, stack, container, etc., which identifies the content, indicates the material symbol (if any) and quantity in hand. It may also record the receipts and issues, the maximum and minimum quantities to be stocked and the re-ordering level.

bit Binary digit. In computing, the smallest possible piece of information that can be stored.

B/L Bill of lading.

black To refuse to deal with or handle, for example, cargo that workers will not handle or a job that trade union members will not apply for, because of an industrial dispute.

black economy Trade and industry that is not officially detected and not reported in official statistics because the participants seek to avoid taxation and other legal requirements.

blackleg A term of abuse often applied generally to any worker reporting to work at a place which is the subject of an industrial dispute and where other workers are on strike. Some would argue that the term applied only to a worker seeking to work in defiance of an official instruction to strike by his or her own trade union, or a non-union worker employed with the specific purpose of breaking a trade-union-supported strike.

blacklist 1. A term given to a list of people known to have defaulted on payments or to have defrauded traders. The list is circulated confidentially among traders for their protection. The practice is declining with the growing use of credit reference agencies who maintain their own blacklists and systems of credit ratings. 2. Any list of traders, countries, etc., with which the compiler of the list is not prepared to trade, e.g. for political or religious reasons.

blacklist certificate A certificate, required by some importing countries, giving evidence that goods have not originated in a blacklisted country, nor carried in a vessel registered in such a country.

blank bill A bill of exchange drawn with out inserting the name of the payee.

blank cheque A cheque complete except for the amount to be paid.

blank credit A letter of credit when no specified sum of money is named upon it.

blank endorsement Writing one's name on the back of a bill or cheque or similar document without stating the name of the person to whom it is being transferred. A bill or cheque so endorsed becomes payable 'to bearer'.

blank transfer A transfer deed with the name of the transferee left blank. Such a transfer may be deposited with a banker when shares etc are being used as a security for a loan.

blending Mixing together different crops or qualities of a product such as tea, coffee or wine to produce a product which the seller believes to be more saleable – or profitable.

blind test A method of testing products by having unidentified samples tested and compared by a panel of consumers.

block release Arrangement under which apprentices or trainees receive training at an educational establishment for a continuous period of some weeks or months uninterrupted by periods of work. Contrast *day release*.

blocked currency A currency that can only be spent within its home country and is not convertible to other currencies.

Blue Book The term commonly applied to 'the CSO Blue Book, United Kingdom National Accounts', published by the Central Statistical Office of the UK.

blue chips The ordinary shares of first class industrial companies.

blue collar Relating to industrial factory work, as in *blue collar worker* and *blue collar pay*.

blueprint A precise plan, drawing or specification.

blue-sky laws (USA) Laws designed to protect investors from investing in worthless securities.

Board 1. The directors of a private or a public

company. 2. The managing group of an organization.

bona fide In good faith, honestly with no intention to defraud or mislead.

bond 1. A deed whereby one party agrees to pay a sum of money or series of sums at a fixed period or periods or on the happening of certain events. Bonds are frequently issued by governments or organizations in return for loans. 2. The term has become widely used to refer to government loan stock whether or not this is in the form of a bond. The feature of government stock is that it pays interest at either a fixed rate or at a stated rate linked to some definite index of price movements. 3. Holding and warehousing goods under the supervision of Customs and Excise until duties have been paid. Goods held 'in bond' are termed *bonded goods*.

bonded stores Dutiable goods intended for use on board ship and, therefore, permitted to be released from bonded warehouses free of duty.

bonded warehouses Storehouses whose owners have secured an approved bond guaranteeing their payment of all duties due on goods stored. Goods stored 'in bond' are subject to strict Customs and Excise supervision but may be sold, blended, re-packed or otherwise modified before release into the distribution system.

bonus 1. A special allowance, premium or present. 2. Share of profits to those entitled to participate in them as 'bonus dividend' to shareholders in a highly profitable year and the payment made to 'with profits' or 'participating' life or endowment assurance policyholders.

bonus shares Shares distributed to shareholders, without any payment, as a capitalization of profits.

book debts Payments outstanding to a business and often classed as 'good', 'doubtful' or 'bad' according to the firm's assessment of the probability of payment.

book-keeping The term usually used to describe the routine work of recording and classifying the financial transactions of a business and preparing the final accounts. The term 'accounting' implies some degree of interpretation of the accounts, financial analysis and decision making.

boom A sustained rise in activity or value, e.g. an economic boom – a period of rising business activity; stock market boom – a major and sustained rise in share values.

boot To start up a computer by loading information, e.g. from a disk.

BOTAC British Overseas Trade Advisory Council. Drawn from members of the *BOTB* and representatives of industry and commerce it has a watching brief on the activities and services of the BOTB and is a two-way channel of communication between British business firms and the BOTB.

BOTB British Overseas Trade Board. The principal British government agency for promoting UK trade interests.

bottomry The mortgage of a ship, e.g. to effect repairs away from its home port.

bought in Bought back for the original owners at an auction, usually because of the failure of bidding to reach the previously advised *reserve price*.

bought out Goods bought or obtained from sources outside the firm.

bought notes and sold notes The written confirmation of agreed sale details exchanged between merchants or brokers.

bourse A widely used European term for a stock exchange or money market.

B/P Bills (of exchange) payable.

B/R Bills (of exchange) receivable.

brainstorming A group method for stimulating ideas by encouraging concentrated and creative thinking.

brand A trade mark. The popular association of branding with quality is derived from early marks which did denote quality standards and were 'branded' (burnt) on to wooden casks or cases.

brand leader The brand of a particular type of goods that has the largest market share.

brand loyalty Preference shown by customers for a particular brand of a good.

breakage An allowance for things broken.

break-even analysis A method of comparing profiles of costs and revenues to determine the time or quantity of sales required before the latter exceed the former – this time or quantity being the *break-even point*. The costs and revenues may be shown graphically on a *break-even chart*.

breaking bulk 1. To open a consignment or parcel for the purpose of taking samples or selling part. 2. To buy goods in bulk for resale in smaller lots. 3. In shipping, the opening of a hold and commencement of unloading.

break-up value The value of the total assets, less liabilities, of a firm if it were to cease trading and its assets sold as separate items.

bridging loan Loan for a short period when the purchase of one asset, such as a house, precedes the sale of another which it is intended to replace.

brief 1. A short account of a client's case for the instruction of counsel. 2. Instruct, retain a barrister. 3. The military sense of giving a set of instructions to subordinates is some times used in business management.

broad money The national stock of money as defined by one of the measures which embrace a wide range of liquid assets in the financial system. In the UK such measures would include M3 and PSL2 (private sector liquidity 2). Contrast *narrow money*.

broker A specialist agent who acts as intermediary between buyer and seller and may act for either, or, in some markets, for both.

brokerage The earnings, based usually on the value of business transacted, of the broker and often in the form of a percentage commission.

B/S Bill of sale.

BSI British Standards Institution. The authorized body in Britain for establishing product safety and quality standards and encouraging business to improve these standards. See also *kitemark*.

bucket shop 1. A colloquial term applied to firms which operate outside normal market institutions and which, therefore, cannot be relied upon to behave according to the standards of the regular market. 2. More generally, an institution operating outside official market bodies, offering legitimate but cut-price services such as cheap air tickets.

budget 1. A projected account of likely or desired future costs and revenues. 2. The amount of money available for spending within a specified period.

budget centre Part of a firm for which budgets are prepared as part of a system of budgetary control.

budgetary control A management control system based on projected accounts prepared in detail. Performance can then be measured against these projections during the budgeted period. Any divergence from the projections can be identified and investigated and measures taken either to return to the desired path or amend the projections.

buffer A computing term for a temporary store for data which is being transferred between devices. It is normally used to accommodate the difference in the rate at which the two devices can handle data during the transfer .

buffer stock Goods or materials held in reserve to ensure that a failure to produce sufficient work-in-progress at one stage of production will not delay subsequent stages.

bug In computing, an error or mistake in a program or a system or a fault in the hardware.

bulk cargo Such cargo as is not in separate bags or bales. The bulk cargo is usually all one commodity such as wheat or oil.

bulk carrier A vessel designed for the carriage and rapid loading and unloading of bulk cargo.

bulk material Material not in unit form directly suited to the work in hand, e.g. bar, tube and sheet steel and material measured only by weight or volume.

bull A speculator who contracts to buy stocks or shares in the expectation of being able to sell them at a higher price before the next settlement. Because a bull is one who anticipates a rise in prices a *bull market* is the term given to a market which is showing a trend towards rising prices.

bullion Gold or silver in lump form, i.e. not coined or, if coined, treated as lump metal and not as currency.

burden See *indirect cost*.

bureau The French word for office. In English the term frequently indicates an independent office from which can be hired specialist services, materials or people. Hence *employment bureau*, a place from which workers may be hired and *computer bureau* where computer hardware, software or skill may be hired.

bureau de change A place where currency can be exchanged.

business agent 1. (USA) A labor union employee representing the 'local' or branch in negotiation. 2. (UK) One who acts on behalf of another in business matters.

business cycle An observed tendency for industrial and commercial activity to move in a series of booms and slumps over a period of years.

business interruption insurance Insurance against loss of business caused by events such as fire or flood as opposed to the direct damage to assets caused by such events. Also known as *consequential loss* insurance.

Business Monitor A series of official British government publications notable for detailed statistical material on specific industries.

business system A set of related components which

may consist of hardware, software, documentation and manual procedures for supporting business activities. Generally the activities will cover one or more of the six main areas of business information, personnel, sales, purchasing, operations, administration and finance.

buyers' market A market in which sellers exceed buyers so that the latter are in a good position to secure bargains.

buyers over A market situation, especially in the UK stock exchanges, where buyers exceed sellers.

buying in If the seller has not delivered his securities to the buyer on the due date, the latter can enforce delivery by buying in against the seller and he would be responsible for all charges and expenses the buyer might incur in getting delivery of his purchase. The time allowed and the manner of enforcing delivery vary on the exchanges according to the rules by which the members are governed.

by-law A regulation made by a public body or a private law or order made by any society, corporation or company. A law with a strictly local or limited application as opposed to the general law of the land.

by-product A product which is produced in the course of manufacturing or processing another.

byte In computers, a unit of information consisting of a fixed number of *bits*.

C

C10 One of the most commonly used import entry forms for goods entering the UK. It is required by Customs and for trade statistics purposes.

C273 One of the most commonly used export pre-entry forms for goods to be exported from the UK. It is required by Customs and for trade statistics purposes.

C/A Capital account. The account that shows the liability or responsibility of an organization to its owner or owners on the assumption that the organization is a separate entity, i.e. has an existence separate from that of its owners.

CAA Civil Aviation Authority. The air licensing and regulatory body of the UK.

C/D Cash against documents. A method of payment in foreign trade in which a bank, acting on behalf of the exporter releases documents, necessary to claim goods, to an importer, on payment of the agreed price.

C & F Cost and freight. A price term signifying that the price includes the cost of goods loaded on board ship, plus cost of freight to the agreed point of delivery in the buyer's country.

cable transfer A term sometimes used to refer to the transfer of money between countries using the telegraph system. See *telegraphic transfer* and *express international money transfer*.

CAD Cash against documents. A payment system under which a bank in the exporter's country is authorized to make an immediate payment to the exporter on receipt of satisfactory documents showing that goods have been shipped to the importer making the payment.

call 1. A demand for payment of an instalment due on shares or stock when only part of the capital has been paid on allotment and the balance is payable in one or a series of further payments. 2. A stock exchange term meaning that by paying so much per cent the *option* is given of buying so much stock at a fixed price on a certain day. 3. In the short term money market, to demand repayment of a loan lent *at call*, i.e. repayable without notice.

call money Money, repayable without notice, lent between the financial institutions operating in the short term money market.

callable bond A redeemable bond, one that the issuer stipulates may be repaid on demand at some stage.

called bond A bond that has been called in for repayment and on which interest is no longer payable.

called-up capital The amount which the company has required shareholders to pay on the shares issued.

Candlemas Day One of the Scottish *quarter days*, 2nd February.

CAP The Common Agricultural Policy of the European Community, a system of regulating production and prices of a range of farm products within the European Community.

capital 1. The money invested in an organization and used to carry on that organization's activities, e.g. to purchase the physical assets needed to conduct its affairs. Also known as *financial capital*. 2. The physical assets or store of human knowledge and skill used to carry on a productive activity, one of the basic *factors of production* identified in economics. Also known as *physical and human capital*.

capital account See *C/A*.

capital budget A budget for capital items such as for the acquisition and disposal of fixed assets.

capital budgeting (especially USA) The analysis and appraisal of capital expenditure projects as an aid to management decisions. See *investment appraisal*.

capital employed All moneys that are effectively employed in the operation of a business.

capital expenditure Moneys spent on acquiring *fixed assets*.

capital gains Appreciation in the value of assets.

capital gains tax A tax, used by a number of

governments, on the capital gains of individuals. In the UK, capital gains by legal corporations are subject to corporation tax.

capital goods Fixed assets with a long life and which are instrumental in producing other goods.

capital intensive A production process that employs a high proportion of capital (machines, etc.) to labour.

capital market The institutions and organizations specializing in the supply of new capital to firms and to dealings in the financial securities thereby created.

capital rationing A situation where a firm has insufficient funds for all its desirable capital expenditure and must, therefore, choose between projects.

capital receipt Money received from the sale of a fixed asset.

capital structure The distribution of a firm's capital by way of ordinary shares, debentures, etc.

capital transfer tax A tax on transfers of wealth either on death or during the lifetime of the donor. In the UK it subsumes estate duty.

capitalization The act of converting into capital, e.g. 'capitalization of profits' when undistributed profits are converted into unpaid capital by the issue of *bonus shares*. Such an issue is also known as a *capitalization issue*.

car tax (UK) An *ad valorem* tax levied on new cars.

carnet A permit authorizing a stated form of transit or temporary residence.

carriage The charge made for conveying goods from one place to another, especially by rail.

carrier Person or firm in the business of carrying goods from one place to another.

carry back To use a tax allowance for one period to offset a tax liability from an earlier period.

carry over A stock exchange term for postponing the settlement of an account from one settling day to another, *contango* or *backwardation* being charged or allowed for the accommodation. Similar arrangements are usually possible on other organized exchanges operating an account system whereby all transactions within an accounting period are normally settled on a particular settlement day.

carrying trade A term sometimes used to describe the transport industry.

cartage The charge made by inland surface carriers for the carriage of goods.

cartage note A statement of the amount of cartage.

cartel An organized combination of suppliers of a particular good or service. Its objectives include the regulation of production and price. OPEC, the oil producing states' cartel, is probably the best known example.

case In the wine and spirit trade a case is deemed to contain twelve bottles of standard size.

cash 1. Any instrument of payment that the payee can convert to his or her own use without incurring a significant charge or having to wait for a significant period of time. For example, a trader in the open economy quoting a 'cash price' usually means the price applying for full, immediate payment by notes, coin or approved cheque, but not for payment in instalments, after a period of credit or by credit card. 2. Especially in the *black economy*, bank notes or coin only. Here the trader may quote two prices, the lower being for payment in cash, the higher for payment by cheque for which account may have to be made to the revenue authorities.

cash account The account showing an organization's payments and receipts. These normally include cheques as well as notes and coin and may include other forms of credit transferred through the banking system.

cash and carry A term usually applied to a wholesale establishment where retailers select their own goods from open displays, pay cash on exit and take the goods away in their own vehicles.

cash book A book containing a record of money paid and received.

cash card A card enabling bank customers to obtain bank notes from automatic cash dispensing machines.

cash credit 1. An agreement made by a bank permitting persons to draw on the bank sums up to a specified amount, interest being charged on the amount actually drawn on a daily basis. 2. A credit, made up entirely of notes and coin, paid into a bank.

cash discount A reduction in the quoted price made in return for payment within a stipulated period.

cash flow The time sequence of a firm's money payments and receipts over a given period. This has an important bearing on the firm's ability to meet its debts when required to do so. A cash flow projection is often a major part of an appraisal (especially by a bank) of a proposed new or expanded undertaking, particularly when this is dependent on borrowings.

cash-on-delivery service A service offered by a carrier such as the Post Office whereby goods are sent to an address but only handed over on receipt of a cash payment.

casting vote The additional vote that may be allowed to the chairman of a meeting to permit a decision when votes are evenly weighted on either side. By custom the chairman is expected to favour a position of 'no change' in such a situation.

casual worker One who is employed on an irregular or occasional basis.

catalogue, catalog 1. A list, in book or booklet form, of goods with descriptions, often with illustrations and detailed references to facilitate ordering and locating prices if these are on a separate list. 2.

A list of files in a computer's memory system, e.g. on a disk.

causa proxima An abbreviation of *causa proxima, non remota spectatur*. A reference to the principle that the immediate and not a remote cause should be sought in determining liability for a loss or event. See *proximate cause*.

caveat emptor The legal principle of 'let the buyer beware'. This basic trading principle that the seller is not obliged to volunteer information detrimental to the goods or services offered for sale is much modified by legislation in many countries including the USA and the European Communities.

CBD Cash before delivery.

CBI The Confederation of British Industry, a major organization representing employers and management in the private and the public sectors of the economy of the United Kingdom.

CCCN Customs Co-operation Council Nomenclature. The standard international classification of goods for customs tariff purposes.

c/d Cleared.

Ceefax The *teletext* service of the British Broadcasting Corporation. It transmits data along with the normal television programme transmissions. A teletext decoder is needed in addition to the normal television receiver.

census An official, systematic enumeration and

survey of the whole or a defined part of the population for the purpose of obtaining information that would not be available by any other means. Governments conduct censuses in relation to production and distribution organizations as well as the general population.

central bank A bank set up or officially associated with the government of a country to perform a number of functions, including, for example, the administration of government borrowings, acting as lender of last resort to the country's financial system, advising on and implementing monetary policy and the supervision and regulation of the country's banking system.

central processing unit (CPU) That part of a computing system that actually performs the computations and other computing processes.

certificate A testimony in writing of something having been done, or a document granting the holder some particular privilege or reward.

certificate of deposit A document, payable to order or bearer, issued by a bank in return for money deposited for a fixed period. The certificate may be used as a security for a loan if the holder requires money before the repayment date.

certificate of health A documentary requirement of certain importing countries in respect of live animals, meat and hides.

certificate of incorporation A certificate granted to a company after satisfactory completion of formalities, stating that it has been duly registered and is now incorporated under the British Companies Acts.

certificate of inspection A documentary requirement of some importing countries. It is designed to ensure that goods conform to the country's required standards.

certificate of insurance See *insurance certificate*.

certificate of origin A certificate sometimes required by an importing country to prove that goods originate from a particular country. The certificate may be needed because of import duty or quota requirements of the importing country. In the UK such certificates are issued by the Chambers of Industry and Commerce.

certificate of quality A document required by some importing countries in respect of the precise strength of chemical content of goods.

certificated bankrupt A person who, after having been made bankrupt, holds a certificate from the Court stating that his or her debts have been cancelled by the Court.

certified cheque See *marked cheque*.

certified transfer A transfer form which bears an endorsement by the registrar or secretary of a company or secretary of a stock exchange, stating that share certificates to meet the transfer have been duly lodged. They are used mainly when a person sells a part holding of shares.

CET The common external tariff (of the European Communities).

C/F Carried forward.

chamber of commerce also

chamber of industry and commerce A local association of business people and representatives of business firms. Its purpose is to promote the interests of members by a very wide variety of means and to provide specialist services and facilities to members. There are close links with other similar bodies at home and in foreign countries. In the UK each local body is a separate, independent organization but in many countries, including some States of the USA, there are close links with government authorities and in some countries the chambers of commerce are completely State owned and controlled.

chamber of trade A body similar to a chamber of commerce and in some areas of the UK amalgamated with the chamber of commerce, but whose members are primarily retail organizations.

charge account See *account*.

charge card A card which enables the holder to purchase goods and services with the price charged to his or her account with the card company. The holder pays the card company's account in full at agreed intervals there being no provision for payment by instalments. Contrast *credit card*.

charge hand A worker with some supervisory responsibility.

charter 1. A grant from the British Crown conferring some special rights, powers or privileges upon public companies, corporations, institutions and the like, upon certain stipulated conditions being fulfilled. 2. (USA) The articles of a corporation. 3. The hiring of a vessel or aircraft.

chartered bank A bank which trades under a special charter granted by the British Crown.

chartered company A company which trades under a special charter from the British Crown as opposed to being registered under the Companies Acts.

charter party A contract made by or on behalf of the owners of a ship and the *charterer* (hirer) for the hiring of a vessel or part of her, for a certain period or voyage at an agreed rate. A charter for single voyage is a *voyage charter*, one for a specified period is a *time charter*.

chartist One who makes decisions relating to the purchase or sale of stock exchange securities on the basis of charts of stock and/or share price movements.

chattels Property other than freehold land. Leasehold land is called *chattels real*, other property *chattels personal*.

cheap money Money is said to be 'cheap' when real rates of interest (interest rates after allowing for inflation rates) are historically low.

check (USA) 1. See *cheque*. 2. The voucher issued by a trading check company permitting the holder to purchase goods or services up to a stated value, from an approved list of retailers. Payment, less an agreed rate of discount, is made to the trader for goods or services supplied, by the check trading company.

check off Deductions by an employer of trade union subscriptions from employees' wages, for forwarding to the union.

check out Place for payment for goods purchased in a self-service store such as a supermarket.

checking account (USA) Same as *current account*.

cheque Equivalent to US *check*. A written order on a bank for the payment of money on demand. The bank on which a cheque is drawn must honour it if the drawer's account contains sufficient funds. A cheque may be made payable to a named payee or to the 'payee's order'. Legally a cheque is a special form of bill of exchange but *acceptance* is not required. Unless *crossed* with the words 'not negotiable' a cheque is a negotiable instrument.

cheque guarantee card or **cheque card** A plastic card, issued by banks to approved personal account holders, carrying the issuing bank's guarantee of payment for a single transaction of a cheque taken from one of its cheque books subject to a stated limit and to the fulfilment of stated conditions.

cheque to bearer A cheque payable on presentation by the holder, unless it is a *crossed cheque* whereupon it must be paid into a bank for collection.

cheque to order A cheque made payable to a named payee or to that payee's order. The cheque may be transferred to another on endorsement by the payee. If it is a *crossed cheque* it must be paid into a bank for collection and any specific instruction on the crossing observed, e.g. payment into a stated bank account.

chip In computing, a small section of a single crystal of *semiconductor*, usually silicon, which is the basis of an integrated circuit.

chop Brand, especially one marked in Chinese or similar characters.

chose in action Intangible property, that is the right to anything not actually in a person's possession, but which can be recovered, if necessary by an action at law. For example, debts, insurance policies, mortgages and other assignable rights.

chose in possession Tangible property, i.e. property which one both has a right to and also has in possession.

chq Cheque.

CIF Cost, insurance, freight. An international price term which indicates that the price includes the costs of goods loaded on board ship, together with the cost of freight and insurance to the agreed point of delivery in the buyer's country.

CIM Conditions for the international carriage of goods by rail.

circulating assets Same as *current assets*.

circulating capital Physical capital which is completely changed in form or consumed by its use, e.g. materials used in production, cash, office stationery.

circulating letter of credit A *letter of credit* addressed to many banks.

circulating medium Recognized means of making payments, e.g. cheques, bank notes, coin, bills of exchange.

City Code on Takeovers and Mergers A set of rules and principles that must be observed in a takeover bid in the UK. The object of the code is to ensure equitable treatment of all shareholders. It is enforced by the Panel on Takeovers and Mergers of the London financial community.

classified advertisement Newspaper advertisement displayed under one of a number of different category headings.

Clayton Act (USA) An antitrust law specifically dealing with exclusive dealing and price discrimination.

clean A term applied to a document which is free of any endorsement or clause indicating that the subject matter of the document is flawed in some way. For example a clean *bill of lading* indicates that there was no apparent damage or loss to goods when the bill was issued and a clean driving licence contains no endorsement noting commission of a driving offence.

clean bill collection An international payments procedure in which a bill of exchange, not accompanied by *shipping documents* is passed to a *collecting bank* for acceptance or immediate payment.

clear a bill To obtain the money in exchange for a bill of exchange.

clearance 1. Of vessels, a permit which must be obtained from Customs before a ship leaves port. It states that all duties have been paid and formalities completed. 2. Of goods, performance by a shipping agent of certain duties connected with the receipt or despatch of goods passing through Customs.

clearing A system of settling accounts between a group of dealers whereby large numbers of individual payments are totalled and the totals set off against each other so that the final liabilities of members to each other can be cleared by just a few payments. Clearings operate in a number of organized markets and exchanges but the best known in the UK is that used by the *clearing banks*, i.e. members of the London Bankers' Clearing House. The banks' clearing system is automated and takes into account local, 'country' (involving a bank branch outside London) and 'town' (payments between the main London offices) clearings. It helps to enable large numbers of cheque and other transfers of credit to take place daily.

clients 1. Persons employing lawyers. 2. Customers of a business.

clock card A card on which a time recording machine records workers' times of entering and leaving a place of work, i.e. *clocking on* and *clocking off*. A similar system may be used to record times of starting and finishing particular jobs.

close company (UK) Defined by Finance Acts, the term concerns tax liabilities and relates, in effect, to a company which is effectively controlled by five or fewer people.

close corporation (USA) A corporation with few shareholders and whose shares are rarely traded.

closed indent See *indent*.

closed shop A place of work where only members of trade unions recognized by the management are permitted to work. In a pre-entry closed shop workers must be union members before being employed. In a post-entry closed shop workers must join a recognized union if not already members.

closing prices In press reports, the closing prices of stocks and shares refer to those transactions which have taken place after the official 'marking' is closed.

CMR Convention Merchandise Routiers. A convention which provides for common rules and procedures in respect of the international carriage of goods across national frontiers by road vehicle, including cases where part of the transit takes place by sea. Hence *CMR consignment note*, the contract document, normally prepared in quadruplicate, and which is required for goods carried under CMR procedures.

C/N Consignment note (transport). *Cover note* (insurance). *Credit note* (commerce).

co Company.

c/o 1. care of 2. *Carry over* (stock exchange).

coasting trade Trade carried out between the home ports only of a country.

COBOL A computer language designed for general business use. From Common Business Orientated Language.

COD Cash on delivery.

code of practice A widely accepted set of procedures, drawn up by, for example, professional or trade associations, trade unions or independent bodies such as *ACAS*.

codetermination Worker participation with management in decision making, especially through a formal system of works councils, joint committees, etc.

codicil An appendix to a will, supplementing, altering, explaining or revoking it.

collateral Extra security, especially in the form of a document giving rights to property, that may be handed over, against the default of a loan or other obligation.

collectables A term used to describe such articles as

postage stamps, antiques or works of art which can be bought and collected for investment purposes.

collecting bank The bank in the importer's country which arranges for payment or acceptance of a bill of exchange not accompanied by shipping documents.

collective bargaining Negotiation on behalf of workers by a trade union.

collective payment by results Collective remuneration for work performed by a group of workers and usually distributed to individual workers on a predetermined basis.

combination A term at one time applied to a trade union but now used to refer to a union of employers formed to the purpose of protecting their own interests or for the regulation of trade and limitation of competition.

combined transport Through delivery of a consignment, by *container*, where more than one method of transport is used, e.g. road vehicle and ship. Hence *combined transport document*, a transport document used when goods are shipped in containers using more than one method of conveyance.

commerce The exchange of articles or services together with the financial and communications services related to such exchange, carried out for money or other payment.

commercial invoice A claim for payment under the terms of a commercial contract with a foreign buyer. It should include full details of the goods, including prices and weight, terms of payment, packing details and shipping marks.

commercial paper Bills of exchange and promissory notes drawn on or issued by industrial firms.

commercial treaty A formal agreement between nations for the regulation or liberalization of trade between them.

commission An employee's or agent's remuneration which is based on the quantity of sales either by a percentage on value of sales or some other agreed method.

commission agent An agent who buys and sells for a principal, especially for foreign principals in return for a percentage return on business transacted.

Commission of the European Communities The civil service of the European Communities, responsible for proposing measures to the Council and Assembly, supervising the Communities' Budget and administering the Communities' policy.

commissioner A lawyer legally authorized to administer oaths.

committee of inspection In bankruptcy or under a deed of assignment, a committee appointed by the creditors from among themselves to watch over the administration of the estate by the trustee and to ensure that the bankrupt's affairs are liquidated in the best interests of those concerned.

commodity A raw material or foodstuff, typically traded in bulk, by weight. In the organized *commodity markets*, often called *commodity exchanges* of London and other major commercial centres, trading is usually controlled by specialized agents termed *commodity brokers*.

common carrier One whose business it is to transport goods and who is prepared to do so for anyone requiring transport services and prepared to pay the usual rates.

common costs Costs which are jointly incurred in the production of several different products or services and which can only be attributed to individual products or services by an arbitrary rule.

common market 1. An arrangement between nation states to allow trade between themselves free of tariffs or other restrictions or with much reduced and simplified frontier administrative arrangements. 2. Common Market The popular name for the European Communities.

common ownership Ownership by two or more people collectively none of whom have separate individual rights to specific parts or the whole.

common stock (USA) Equivalent to the British terms *ordinary stock or shares*.

communication system A system which supports

company promoter

communication facilities such as telephony, transmission of data, and audio and visual conference links between people in different locations.

communications satellite An electronic device encircling the earth. It provides long-distance microwave channels for telephony, data and broadcasts.

Companies Acts A series of Acts of Parliament which provide the statutory framework for the formation, regulation and winding up of companies in the United Kingdom. Acts passed from 1948 to 1984 have been consolidated in the Companies Act 1985. Schedule 1 of this Act identifies *companies limited by guarantee*, *companies limited by shares*, and *unlimited companies*. It also defines *public companies* and *private companies*.

company An association of persons for carrying on a trade or business.

company limited by guarantee A company in which the liability of members is limited to the amount they have guaranteed to pay in the event of liquidation. This is a common structure for non-trading companies such as sports organizations.

company limited by share A company in which the liability of the members is limited to the amount of share capital they have undertaken to subscribe.

company promoter The person or one of a number of persons who carry out the preliminary work necessary to form or float a company but not including those professional advisers such as lawyers and accountants whose services are needed to complete the necessary processes.

company secretary An official of a company, responsible in British law for certain duties such as the keeping of records and making certain returns to the Registrar of Companies.

compensating error A mistake in the accounts which is equalized by another mistake or mistakes and which does not, therefore, show up by a failure to balance and can, therefore, be very difficult to trace and correct.

composite office A term applied to an insurance office which transacts all or most of the main branches of insurance, including, fire, accident and life insurance. Contrast with a *specialist office* that transacts one major class of business only, often life business.

composition A payment of a proportion of each debt instead of a payment in full by a bankrupt or insolvent person.

compound bonus A life assurance term for a bonus or share of profit which, like compound interest, is added to the main sum payable under a policy which is the sum assured, for purposes of future bonus calculation, i.e. bonuses are paid on bonuses. Contrast *simple bonus*.

compound interest Interest which is not paid to a lender when due but added to the principal so that future interest calculations are based on the principal plus accumulated interest, including 'interest on interest'. Contrast *simple interest*.

compounding with creditors Agreeing to a *composition* with creditors who then allow the bankrupt or insolvent person an *acquittance* for the full amount owing.

compulsory purchase The purchase by a public authority, under powers granted in the UK by Parliament, of land or property without the acquiescence of the owner. Hence *compulsory purchase order*, the authority to make a specific purchase.

compulsory winding-up The termination of a company by order of the Court.

computer An electronic machine that receives, stores, transfers information and carries out a range of processes, including calculation very rapidly, in response to programmed instructions.

concessions Grants of certain privileges given by governments to persons, the *concessionaires* to carry out undertakings believed to be in the interest of the nation.

conciliation An attempt to resolve an industrial dispute though the mediation of a third party acceptable to both sides.

conditional order An order to a bank to make a payment provided that a form of receipt is duly signed. As it is a payment subject to conditions and not, therefore a cheque or bill of exchange, the bank may insist on certain safeguards for itself.

conditions of sale The terms and conditions upon which goods are sold by public auction. They are usually printed on catalogues and brought to the attention of potential buyers before buying commences.

confirmation note A slip attached to or sent with an order or contract for the receiver to sign and return as confirmation of receipt and agreement to the contract.

confirmed credit A credit, opened in favour of an exporter by a bank representing the importer and which is confirmed by an advising bank (see *advise*) in the exporter's country. The *confirming bank* will be acting under an irrevocable letter of credit from the importer's home bank. Provided the exporter fulfils all the terms of the credit, payment is received from the confirming bank without any further liability.

confirming house A firm acting as a commission agent in foreign trade, paying exporters and collecting payment from foreign buyers.

conglomerate 1. A holding company with a large number of subsidiaries, especially those acquired through takeovers. 2. A firm with an extremely diversified range of activities.

consequential loss insurance See *business interruption insurance*.

consideration 1. The payment, sacrifice or undertaking made in the formation of a valid legal contract. Each party to a contract must receive a consideration for the contract to be valid. 2. In the stock exchange the money value of the contract transferring shares without taking into account broker's commission, stamp duty and other payments.

consign To forward goods from one place or person to another, the *consignee*. The party sending or authorizing the sending of the goods is the *consignor*.

consignment 1. A batch of goods consigned. 2. Goods forwarded to an agent for sale at the best possible price. 3. Goods forwarded to a customer for use, and hence purchase or return.

consignment account An arrangement in foreign trade whereby an exporter supplies a stock of goods to a foreign buyer sufficient to meet continual demand. Ownership of the goods remains with the exporter until they are sold or for an agreed period. Payment is made according to agreed terms.

consignment note A printed form used when goods are sent by rail, (railway consignment note) or air (air consignment note), giving the forwarding instructions. Also used when goods are sent by ship without a bill of lading. Unlike bills of lading, consignment notes are not full documents of title and not negotiable. An air consignment note is also known as an *air waybill*.

consolidated The term applied to various funds bearing the same or different rates of interest, which have been merged or consolidated into one common debt.

consolidated accounts Accounts of a holding company and its subsidiaries, treating them as one firm.

consols Consolidated annuities, stocks with fixed interest but no stated date of maturity, issued by the British Government.

consortium A number of firms or bodies working together for a single project or enterprise.

constructive dismissal Under British employment law, actions on the part of an employer which may be construed as the effective dismissal of the employee because they change the nature of the work to such an extent that the worker could not reasonably be expected to continue working. An action of this kind might be a major change in work practice involving a serious deterioration in working conditions.

consul A public official appointed by a government to reside in a foreign country to look after the interests of its citizens in that country. A consul has specific commercial responsibilities, including providing advice and assistance to traders of the consul's country, supervising the operation of commercial treaties and, for example, signing consular invoices.

consular invoice Invoices which have been 'visa'd' (seen and signed) by the consul of the country to which they have been shipped. Some countries require such invoices as an essential import document and, in so doing secure an additional import tax because a fee is charged for each document approved by the consul.

consumable stores Indirect material chargeable as overheads. Examples include lubricants, waste and canteen supplies.

consumer durables Goods such as television sets, motor vehicles or freezers, purchased by final consumers for use over a significant period of time.

consumer group An interest or pressure group agitating for some aspect of *consumerism*.

Consumer Price Index A major US index of movements in retail prices.

Consumer Protection Advisory Committee A group which has the duty to advise the Director General of Fair Trading and the Secretary of State for Trade (or Trade and Industry) on matters relating to consumer affairs and trading practices as they affect consumers in the UK.

consumerism A movement that developed from the 1960s onwards to press for various improvements in business practices and services in the interests of the customer, e.g. improved safety standards, after-sales service, customer information and warranties.

container A standardized metal box measuring 8ft (2.4m) high by 8ft (2.4m) wide by either 20ft (6.1m) or 40ft (12.2m) long, with a weight capacity of 3 to 12 tonnes, that greatly facilitates transport and handling by road, rail, sea and air. Air containers may be specially shaped to fit into aircraft.

contango The charge made by jobbers in the stock exchange for carrying over a buying transaction to the next settlement.

contango day The first day of the stock exchange settlement and the day on which arrangements are made by stockbrokers and their clients for carrying over transactions to the next account. See also *making up day*.

contingency An event which cannot be precisely forecast but for which provision must be made. A fund to provide for contingencies is a *contingency fund*.

contingent annuity An annuity payable only in the event of some contingency happening, e.g. someone's death.

contingent liability A liability which can exist definitely only upon the happening of some uncertain event, e.g. the liability of an endorser under a bill of exchange.

continuation Carrying over or deferring the purchase or delivery of securities to the next account.

continuation clause 1. The clause in time marine insurance contracts whereby, for an agreed premium, the underwriters agree to continue cover until the ship reaches port if it is still at sea when the time of cover expires. 2. Generally in insurance policies, a clause obliging the insurer to continue to provide cover after the period already paid for until renewal can be arranged.

continuation rates The charges, *contango* and *backwardation*, made in the stock exchange for carrying over bargains to the next account.

contra A term used in accounting to mean 'against' or 'on the opposite side'.

contraband Prohibited or dutiable goods smuggled into a country.

contract An agreement, especially a legally enforceable agreement.

contract in In the UK, an arrangement whereby members of a trade union do not pay a political levy (if any) to the union unless they personally and specifically opt to do so.

contract note Stock exchange term for the document sent to a client by a stockbroker giving details of a buying or selling transaction completed on the client's behalf.

contract of employment Under UK law the contract assumed to exist between employer and employee. Employment contracts and the employee's right to see a written contract are subject to statute law in Britain.

contract out 1. In the UK, an arrangement whereby members of a trade union automatically contribute to the union's political levy unless they specifically opt not to do so. 2. In the UK, the provision by an employer of a pension scheme for employees which meets the conditions necessary for exemption from the general state pension scheme.

contributed capital Capital received by a company in return for the issue of its shares.

contribution The margin between the sales revenue of an item and the *variable costs* incurred in producing it and hence the amount contributed by the sale towards fixed, overhead expenses and profit. Equivalent of US *contribution margin*.

contributory A person legally liable in actions of contract to make good the default of another, although not necessarily bound to do so by express contract.

control account A total account inserted in a ledger to make it self-balancing. A run of debits and credits is posted to the individual ledger accounts and the total of both or the net value is posted to the control account. The balance of the account should thus always equal the total of the balances on the individual accounts in the subsidiary ledger.

control unit The portion of the *central processing unit* of a computer that contains the *registers* and other elements which provide control of the movement of information between the memory and the calculating or processing units. It thus controls the process whereby program instructions are carried out.

convenience foods Packaged foods prepared in such

a way that they require the minimum of cooking and further preparation by the consumer before being apparently ready and fit for eating.

convenor The senior or principal shop steward in a work establishment. Sometimes used to describe the senior shop steward of one of the main unions with members in the workplace. The term is found frequently in the British engineering industry and the engineering trade unions.

conversion 1. Wrongly disposing of another's property without that person's permission. 2. Changing one thing into another, used especially of industries such as mineral refining, and also currency exchange.

conversion cost The cost of converting raw materials into prepared materials or finished products, exclusive of the cost of the raw materials.

convertible securities Those securities which contain the right to transfer from one form of holding to another, usually from loan to ordinary stock.

conveyance The transfer of property from one person to another and the preparation of the documents and deeds involved in the transfer.

co-operative A business owned and controlled by its working members (worker co-operative) or its customers (customer co-operative) on an equal-share basis, rather than in proportion to the capital contributed by each.

co-partnership A profit-sharing scheme in which the

employees are entitled not only to a share in the profits but also to a voice in the management of the concern.

copy In advertising, the words used in an advertisement.

copyright The sole legal right to publish or reproduce anything that belongs to the author or anyone authorized by the author.

copywriter One who composes advertising copy.

corner To *make a corner* or *corner the market* is to buy up all the available stock of a particular commodity.

corporate database An information computer *database* which holds data concerned with a specific company or organisation.

corporation A body or society authorized by law to act as a single individual and to perpetuate its existence by the admission of new members.

corporation tax A tax on the profits, including capital gains, of UK companies and unincorporated associations except partnerships and certain exempt funds, notably charities, local authorities and trade unions.

cost The value in terms of money of the efforts, utilities, risks and abstinences which comprise the real cost measured in resources. See also *cost, real*.

cost account An account recording revenues and expenditures of cost centres or units for control purposes as distinct from the legal requirement of financial reporting.

cost accounting The establishment of budgets and standard costs and actual costs of operations, processes, departments or products and the analysis of variances and profitability.

cost allocation The distribution of cost to units, processes, services or products in the proportions in which they have incurred it.

cost and freight See *C & F*.

cost-benefit analysis A method of appraising projects, especially public works projects, by calculating monetary values for the various social costs and benefits arising from them and then comparing the results.

cost, insurance and freight See *CIF*.

cost of living index A common term applied to an index of retail prices such as the British All Items Index of Retail Prices and the US Consumer Price Index.

cost plus contract A contract to supply at the cost of production plus a fixed, agreed percentage or fee.

cost plus pricing Any system of pricing in which the price is set at the cost of production plus a *mark-up*.

cost, real The sacrifices that are incurred when resources are used for one undertaking rather than another. For example the real costs of using freehold property would include the rent that could be earned if it were let to another.

cost unit The total cost of goods or services divided by the number of units of the goods or services.

costing The systematic calculation of the costs of producing or providing goods or services.

countertrading A form of trade between countries based on the direct exchange of goods for goods rather than by direct payment by money. It is a form of modern *barter* that has proved useful for a number of countries with currency problems.

counterclaim Action for damages brought by the defendant of a case against the plaintiff, arising out of the same or related events.

counterfoil A detachable tally or memorandum to share certificates, cheques, receipts, etc., containing a record of the issue of the main document and kept by the person issuing it.

counterpart The opposite person or organisation in a foreign exchange deal. A dealer who sells currency three months forward will have a counterpart who buys three months forward.

countersign Add a further signature to a document in order to increase its acceptability.

countervailing duty Import duty imposed by one state on the exports of another in retaliation for duties imposed by the latter on the exports of the former or to compensate for export subsidies granted by the latter.

coupon A note of interest or dividend attached to transferable bonds. Coupon means a 'cutting' and as the dividends fall due the forms are cut off and presented for payment.

coupon sheet A connected series of coupons given in advance with bearer bonds in order that they may be cut off from time to time and presented for payment as the dividends fall due.

court of enquiry A body set up in the UK by the government to investigate and present a formal report on an industrial dispute. It is made up of representatives of employers and trade unions and has an independent chairperson.

covenant An agreement to do a certain thing or to refrain from a certain course of action. Because it usually involves an undertaking on one side with no *consideration* from the person receiving the benefit, it is usually made by means of a deed, under seal.

cover 1. In the stock exchange, a deposit of money or marketable securities given by a client to a broker to provide protection against loss when a speculative transaction is being made. It is sometimes called a *margin*. 2. The amount and extent of protection afforded by an insurance policy. 3. The ratio between the net earnings of a company and its dividend payments.

cover note A form providing evidence of insurance cover pending preparation of the policy.

CPA Critical path analysis. A method of determining

the minimum period of time in which a sequence of events may be completed and of identifying the correct sequence.

craft union A trade union comprising manual workers of a particular skill who may work in a number of different industries.

craftsman A worker who has successfully completed an apprenticeship or, more generally, a skilled worker.

CRE Commission for Racial Equality. The body which, in the UK, has the duty of upholding the law on racial discrimination and generally promoting greater equality of opportunity regardless of ethnic origins.

credit 1. The lending of wealth or capital by one to another, the lender being said to give, and the borrower to receive, credit. 2. An entry in a bank's records increasing the amount of the bank's liability to a customer whose credit is thereby increased. 3. An increase in the liability of a business to a ledger account or its equivalent in computerized accounting. 4. A commercial arrangement under which goods or services are sold to a buyer who undertakes to pay the whole or the balance of the price at an agreed time in the future or by agreed future instalments. Until the full amount agreed has been paid the buyer remains a *debtor* and the seller a *creditor*.

credit account (Equivalent to US *charge account*). An arrangement between a retailer and customer whereby the latter is able to purchase up to a stated value of goods on credit in return for payment at agreed, periodic intervals.

credit agency Also known as a *credit reference agency* this is a commercial organization whose business it is to investigate and keep records of the financial standing and creditworthiness (credit rating) of individuals and firms and sell this information to clients.

credit card A card issued by a financial organization enabling the holder to obtain credit from a large number of suppliers. The suppliers receive payment from the firm issuing the card, the credit card company, less a commission. The card holder pays the card company in accordance with the terms under which the card is issued. This may include payment by instalments. Contrast *charge card*.

credit control Method and system operated by a business whereby it decides whether and to what extent to issue credit and to monitor repayments.

credit limit The extent of credit granted by a firm to its customer or, in the case of a financial organization, to a borrower.

credit line (USA) The equivalent of UK *credit limit*.

credit note A document sent to an account holder stating that the account has been credited with a stated amount.

credit-sale agreement An agreement to sell on the

understanding that payment will be received in instalments. Ownership of the property sold passes immediately to the buyer. Contrast with *hire purchase* where ownership does not pass to the buyer until the option to purchase has been exercised, usually by paying the final instalment.

credit squeeze Government policy instrument involving the restriction of credit throughout the economy, for example, by raising interest rates, reducing credit limits or placing special restrictions on the issue of credit.

credit transfer A transfer of funds from one bank account to another within the banking system.

credit union (USA) An organization for mutual assistance, e.g. among employees of a firm, to provide cheap loans for each other provided out of members' subscriptions.

creditor One to whom another is in debt for goods, cash, etc.

critical path analysis See *CPA*.

CRN Customs registered number. A number which exporters must obtain if they wish to take advantage of the simplified customs procedure available to regular exporters of goods not liable to duty or restriction.

crossed cheque A cheque crossed on the face by two parallel lines, sometimes with instructions such as 'not negotiable' or 'account payee'. Payment of crossed cheques is subject to certain restrictive conditions.

cross currency exposure This refers to the ability of an international organisation to meet its obligations in a currency with the revenue is earns in that currency.

cross-firing Fraudulent use of several bank accounts to obtain cash from one against cheques drawn on others and relying on the fact that cheques take a certain time to clear between banks.

cross rate The rate of exchange derived by expressing the quotations for two currencies in terms of a third. If, say, one pound sterling equals US$1.50 and also equals 12 French francs then the cross rate for dollars and francs is $1 = 8 francs.

cross subsidization The practice, within an organization, of supporting a loss-making activity from the profits made by another, profitable part of the business.

CT Community transit. The term used to refer to the transit documents used for goods traded between members of the European Communities.

CTT Capital transfer tax. See *capital transfer tax*.

cum (Latin) with. Opposite to *ex*, without. A security quoted *cum div* entitles the buyer to the next dividend to become due. *Cum drawing* refers to bonds about to be drawn and consequent benefits such as a premium. *Cum new* or *cum rights* may be used to refer to an allotment of new shares to be distributed to existing shareholders.

cum pref Cumulative preference. Used in respect of *cumulative preference stocks and shares*.

cumulative preference stocks and shares Securities upon which, if the guaranteed dividend cannot be paid in any one year, or any series of years, the dividend accumulates until it can be paid and such accumulated dividend is entitled to payment before any dividend is paid either on the preference or ordinary shares for any succeeding year. In practice any company unable to pay preference dividends for a series of years is likely to have to ask shareholders to forego all or some of these rights as a precondition for a return to profitability.

currency Any qualified accepted medium of exchange or means of payment within a country, including coins, banknotes, cheques and bills of exchange.

currency basket A combination of currencies used as a reference unit of account to facilitate currency valuation, exchange and trade. Two well known currency baskets are the *ECU* and *SDRs*.

currency of a bill The period between the date upon which a bill is drawn and that upon which it becomes due. When a bill is payable 'after sight' the currency begins from the date of acceptance. When drawn 'after date' it starts from the date of the bill.

currency swap An arrangement whereby two international organisations exchange currencies for an agreed period.

current asset An asset, such as stock or a short-term investment, which will be converted into cash fairly shortly by a firm in the normal course of business.

current cost accounts Accounts using asset values which reflect changes brought about by *inflation* and other causes since the time of acquisition. Contrast *historic cost*.

current liability An amount of money which is due to be paid by the organization in the near future.

current ratio The ratio of the current assets of a business to its current liabilities.

cursor A symbol on a computer display screen that indicates the active position, i.e. the position at which the next character to be entered will be displayed. The symbol is often a small rectangle or the underline character and frequently it is made to blink or flash so that it can easily be distinguished within a screen of text. It can be manipulated by *cursor control keys*.

Custom house A place appointed by the Government for the purpose of imposing and collecting such duties on imports and exports as are authorized by the laws of the country.

custom and practice In British labour relations this term is used to describe those working and employment practices which, though not formally agreed, have come, through usage, to be widely accepted as part of the arrangements between employer and employees.

customs Taxes imposed on imports and exports as authorized by the laws of the country.

customs and excise duties The taxes levied on certain imports and, rarely, exports (customs) or on certain manufactured goods, in the UK chiefly alcohol (excise).

customs declaration 1. A statement to the Customs authorities listing and detailing goods being imported. 2. A form giving details of a parcel to be sent abroad.

customs entry A list given to the Customs authorities showing details of goods imported or exported. Import declarations are known as *import entries* and export declarations, which usually have to be made before goods are shipped, are known as *pre-entries*.

customs tariff The official list of customs duties payable.

customs union An arrangement between two or more countries removing or reducing customs and other barriers to the free movement of traded goods between them.

CWO Cash with order.

cy près As nearly as possible, a term used in connection with trusts. If, for some reason the terms of a trust cannot be carried out exactly the Courts may order that these terms are carried out *cy près*.

D

D/A Documents against acceptance. A method of payment in foreign trade in which documents enabling an importer to claim goods are released when a bill of exchange is accepted by the importer or on the importer's behalf by a bank.

'D' notice A formal request issued by the Defence Press and Broadcasting Committee to editors, asking them not to publish certain information in the interests of national security.

daisywheel The print wheel of an electronic typewriter.

data 1. A collection of figures, facts or information available for analysis. 2. A general term for numbers, digits, characters and symbols which are accepted, stored and processed by a computer.

data bank Collection of facts and information, usually held on computer, for use by commerce, industry, government or research bodies.

data management A computing term normally used to refer to *systems* that manipulate data automatically and present it in a form which enables users to concentrate on interpreting its logical properties.

data processing Recording and reworking, usually by computer, large amounts of information into various pre-planned forms.

database A collection of interrelated data values of such a nature that they might be represented as a number of files but not as a single file. The use and structure of data stored in a database need not be dependent upon any specific application.

day books Accounts recording the details of day-to-day, especially sales, transactions.

day release A system of training whereby employees attend a college or other educational establishment away from the place of work for one day per week.

day-to-day loans or **day-to-day accommodation** or **day-to-day money** Sums borrowed by financial institutions for a period of a day but renewable by agreement.

days' sight Days after 'sight' of a bill, i.e. after its presentation for acceptance.

DCF Discounted cash flow. See *discounted cash flow*.

dead account The money or securities held to the credit or on behalf of a deceased bank account holder.

dead freight Freight payable for space booked but not used.

dead loans Loans which have not been paid at the agreed time or for which no time for payment has been specified.

dead rent A fixed rent payable under a mining lease whether or not the mine is being worked.

dead security Certain mines, industrial properties, quarries, etc., which are worth nothing as security if not being worked.

dead stocks 1. Unsaleable goods that do not contribute to the turnover of the firm. 2. In agriculture, buildings, machinery, etc as opposed to livestock.

dead weight 1. The weight of heavy cargo that brings a ship down to the maximum *load line*. 2. Heavy goods carried in the bottom of a ship to steady it. 3. (USA) The unladen weight of a road or rail vehicle. Equivalent of UK *tare*.

dealer A person dealing on own account and not as an agent of another.

dear money A situation existing when very high rates of interest have to be paid on loans even when these are supported by first class securities.

death duty A tax levied on the value of property belonging to a person who has died. In the UK this duty has been replaced by *capital transfer tax*.

debenture A security issued by a company or corporation entitling the holder to a fixed interest payment. The term is commonly applied in the UK to loan stocks which are secured by a floating charge on the assets of the organization and with a prior claim on the assets. Debentures are usually redeemable by the issuer. *Mortgage debentures* are secured by a mortgage on property owned by the issuer.

debenture bond (USA) Equivalent to *unsecured loan stock* in the UK.

debit A charge against a person or account.

debit note A notification of a charge against a supplier resulting from an error, the return of goods or some other agreed cause.

debt The amount owed by one, the *debtor* to another the *creditor*.

debt capital also **loan capital** Money loaned to a firm for a considerable period of time (at least a year). Providers of debt capital are creditors of the firm and normally receive interest as opposed to shareholders who have ownership rights, including the right to a division of profits.

debt collection The process of recovering moneys owed by debtors, a process often undertaken by a specialist agency.

debt ratio The ratio between the debt capital of a firm and its total capital, both debt and *equity*.

debt servicing The payment of interest on a debt.

debugging The tracing and removal of errors from a computer program or the elimination of faults from any system.

declaration of solvency In UK company law, the formal, sworn statement by the directors of a company on its winding up that all debts will be repaid in a given period of time not exceeding a year.

deed 1. A legal transaction. 2. The written document,

under hand and seal, being the evidence of such a transaction.

deed of arrangement In bankruptcy, an arrangement made by deed by an insolvent debtor for the benefit of the whole of the creditors.

deed of assignment A deed by which a debtor gives up the whole of his or her property for the benefit of the creditors.

deed of inspectorship A deed under which an insolvent trader places his or her business into the hands of the creditors who appoint trustees, called inspectors, for the purpose of carrying on the business or winding it up for their general benefit.

deed of partnership A deed outlining the rights and relationship of the members of a partnership as agreed between them.

default 1. Failure to pay a debt. 2. Failure to perform a duty.

default value The value that a computer will take automatically when an entry is omitted.

defendant A person accused or sued and who opposes the charge.

deferred annuity An annual payment for a fixed number of years, or for life, commencing at the end of an agreed period.

deferred bonds Bonds which bear a rate of interest which gradually increases until a fixed specified rate has been reached.

deferred charges Prepaid items of expense, such as rates, taxes, insurance premiums, rent and patent fees which, because they have not been wholly 'consumed' in the current accounting period have unabsorbed balances to be carried forward to the ensuing periods.

deferred credits Income received during the current period on account of the ensuing period to which the items are to be credited.

deferred stock or shares Stock or shares which do not entitle the holders to any dividend until a fixed rate has been paid on the preference and ordinary shares.

deficiency A shortfall; an excess of liabilities over assets, or of expenditure over income.

deficiency, (or surplus) account In the statement of affairs of a bankrupt, an account of changes in the assets and liabilities in the twelve months preceding a receivership against that bankrupt.

deflation Strictly, a reduction in price levels throughout the economy. Today, the term is frequently used to refer to a stagnation or reduction in economic activity, usually initiated by government policy and intended to reduce the amount of money, credit, or demand in the economy.

del credere An undertaking made by an agent, in return for additional payment or commission, guaranteeing the payment to the principal for all goods sold on commission, whether or not payment is received from the buyer.

delegate To entrust the performance of a part of one's own duties to another.

delivered at frontier An international price term used chiefly in relation to goods transported by rail or road. The seller pays all costs up to the point where the goods arrive at the frontier and before the 'customs border' of the country specified in the contract.

delivered duty paid An international price term which is accompanied by the destination for delivery. If this is stated to be the buyer's premises and there is no exclusion of any specific tax then the seller agrees to pay all costs, including all import duties and taxes, up to the point of delivery at the buyer's location. This is the maximum possible liability and is at the other end of the scale from *ex works*.

delivery note A note giving details of a consignment of goods and delivered with the goods. The signature of the receiver on the delivery note provides evidence of delivery.

demand 1. A request for payment. 2. The quantity of goods or services that customers are willing and have the purchasing power to purchase. 3. The quantities of goods or services that are likely to be purchased at various prices within a specified range. 4. on demand, without any period of notice.

demand deposit Money deposited with a bank and which can be withdrawn without notice.

demand draft A bill of exchange payable on demand and which does not require accepting.

demarcation dispute A dispute between two or more trade unions each claiming that a particular work task is the exclusive right of its own members.

demurrage A daily charge made by the owners of ships or barges for their detention by a charterer beyond a specified time.

Department of Employment A department of the British government responsible in particular for manpower planning, youth and adult vocational and skills training, policy on racial and sexual equality at work, some aspects of unemployment and the gathering of employment statistics.

Department of Trade and Industry A department of the British government, formerly separate departments of trade and industry, having as its main responsibilities company and commercial law, commercial policy and foreign trade, regional policy, government assistance to industry and some nationalized firms and industries.

department store A store organized on the basis of separate trading departments each of which specializes in a particular class of goods.

departmentalization The organization of a business and the classification of its expenditure, functions and operations on the basis of departments, production centres and services.

dependencies Assets likely to accrue but which cannot now be exactly determined. Examples include profits and dividends on investments.

depletion The exhaustion which takes place in natural resources when raw materials are extracted from mines, quarries and similar sources and when the fertility of agricultural land is diminished.

deposit Money placed by a *depositor* with bankers and others on agreed terms and conditions.

depot A place of deposit for goods, a store, a military station, a transport terminus.

depreciation 1. The loss of value of an asset due to the passage of time, normal use or obsolescence. 2. The allowance made in the accounts for this loss of value and calculated according to one of a number of accounting conventions. 3. A fall in the rate at which the national currency trades against foreign currencies in the foreign exchange markets. 4. A fall in the purchasing power of money, i.e. its exchange value in relation to goods and services.

devaluation A significant reduction in the rate at which the national currency trades against other currencies, especially when this is brought about by deliberate government action.

devastavit A breach of trust involving loss to the estate.

development area or region In the UK, an area which

devisee One to whom real estate is bequeathed by another, the *devisor*.

dies non A day on which, because of some particular circumstance or event, no business is transacted.

differences A stock exchange term relating to those bargains where the operator does not intend to take up or deliver the stocks traded but is speculating for the difference in price on the settling day.

differential (wage) The amount by which one wage scale or the wages of a particular occupation exceed or fall short of another.

differential piece rate system A method of remuneration in which a scale of quantities is first determined and piece rates fixed for various quantities on a sliding scale.

digital computer A computer in which real information and data are represented and processed by a system of digits. Contrast *analog computer*.

dilution 1. Of equity, an increase in the number of shares in the firm without an equivalent increase in assets or earning power and causing a proportionate fall in the value of the old shares. 2. Of labour, the substitution of unskilled or semi-skilled workers for skilled labour.

direct cost In cost accounting, all expenditure which

can reasonably be attributed exclusively to the production of particular goods or services.

direct debit Method of making periodic payments through a bank account whereby the payee authorizes the recipient to have the money paid directly from the former's account to the latter's, on presentation of the latter's *mandate* to the bank.

direct departmental expenses With the exception of materials and wages, all items of cost which can be charged directly to specific departments. Examples might include rent, rates, heating and lighting charges and telephone charges.

direct expense With the exception of materials and wages not forming part of the normal production overhead, all items of cost that are incurred on specific products, production units or services.

direct goods account An account to which are charged materials purchased for a specific cost unit.

direct mail advertising Advertising material sent by post to potential customers.

direct profit Sales revenue from a product less the *direct costs* attributable to that product.

direct sale Sale made by a manufacturer to the final consumer without the agency of any intermediary such as a retailer.

direct tax Tax imposed upon and directly payable by individuals or corporations.

director 1. The chief manager of an undertaking or clearly identifiable part of an organization. The title is often qualified to indicate the extent or nature of responsibility, e.g. managing director, personnel director. 2. Member of a Board of Directors of a limited company which may be a subsidiary of another. Directors of subsidiaries will, in effect, be appointed by the dominant company. Directors of the 'main board' of the parent company will be subject to election by the shareholders in accordance with the provisions of the company's *articles of association*. Directors may be full-or part-time.

directorate 1. The office of a director. 2. The body of directors.

Director-General of Fair Trading A senior British official, the head of the Office of Fair Trading. See *OFT*.

dirty money An extra payment made to workers for handling goods of an objectionable nature.

discharge 1. Carry out or fulfil an obligation or duty. 2. Release from an obligation. 3. Terminate an employee's employment.

discharged bankrupt A bankrupt who has received a discharge from the Court, i.e. has been released from the restrictions imposed as a consequence of bankruptcy. The Court will have to have been convinced that all reasonable efforts have been made to settle debts. Any remaining debts would usually be wiped out.

disclaimer A statement, clause in a deed, contract, etc., renouncing claims, responsibility, duties or powers.

discount 1. Reduction from a list, catalogue or retail price, often given for payment in cash, for bulk order or to members of the trade. 2. To sell to another the right to collect a debt at a later date, e.g. to discount a bill of exchange whereby the bill is discounted for some fraction of the amount payable. 3. At a discount, e.g. of shares, means that the price of something is below its *nominal value* or *par value*.

discount house A financial institution a major part of whose business is to discount bills of exchange and treasury bills.

discount market That part of the market in finance which is concerned with short-term borrowing and which is largely in the hands of discount houses, bill brokers and those banks prepared to discount commercial bills of exchange and treasury bills.

discount rate The rate of interest employed in a discounting operation, e.g. discounting bills of exchange or investment appraisal.

discount store Retail establishment, usually large and specializing in consumer durables, offering goods at cut prices.

discounted cash flow The general term applied to those systems of *investment appraisal* (capital budgeting) in which future streams of costs and revenues are discounted to their present value equivalents, the amount of discount depending on the rate of discount chosen and the length of period between the present and the time of anticipated payment.

discretionary order An order sent by a stock exchange operator to a broker giving instructions as to the value of stock to purchase but leaving it to the broker's discretion as to what stock is bought.

dishonour When applied to a bill of exchange this means to refuse to accept a bill or to fail to pay as required by the terms of an acceptance.

disintermediation The action of borrowers and lenders in financial markets of by-passing the usual financial intermediaries such as banks or creating credit between themselves without any financial agencies or obtaining credit from banks and other financial institutions in ways which avoid official credit control regulations.

disk or diskette In computing, a flat circular magnetic surface used for the storage of information. The information is written and read by means of a *disk drive*.

dispatch note A note from the sender to the receiver of goods to inform the latter that the goods have been sent.

display advertising An advertisement placed in a printed publication and designed to catch the attention of readers.

dissolution 1. Formal ending of the existence of a company, in the UK three months after the completion of the winding up of its affairs. 2. Ending of a partnership, by agreement, or because death, retirement or other cause has brought the existing partnership agreement to an end.

distrain To seize goods for debt.

distrainor One who distrains goods for debt.

distraint The seizure of goods for debt.

distress 1. In law, the act of distraining goods. 2. To chip and mark reproduction furniture to give it the appearance of age.

distressed The term used in the antique trade to indicate damage and marking suffered in the course of time.

distribution The activities involved in moving goods from the manufacturer or importer to the final customer, including storage and warehousing, transport, customer relations and credit control as well as wholesale and retail selling.

distribution mix The pattern of distribution used by a manufacturer, different types of goods calling for different methods of distribution.

distribution network The wholesalers, retailers, merchants, agents and others who participate in the distribution of goods between manufacturers or importers and customers throughout the economy.

distributive trades The sectors of economic activity whose business is distribution.

distributor A firm or individual acting as an intermediary between manufacturer or importer and customer.

diversification Expansion of the range of goods and services produced by a firm into other related or unrelated industries or markets.

divestment 1. Transfer of the ownership and control of part of a firm's activities to another, independent organization. This may be undertaken under compulsion as part of a government's antitrust policy. 2. Transfer of the whole or part of a firm's activities from its home country to another country.

dividend 1. Interest payments on securities issued by the British government. 2. A periodical division and distribution of profits among the shareholders of companies. 3. Any instalment paid to the creditors from a bankrupt's estate.

dividend mandate A stockholder's authorization for the company to pay dividend direct to a specified bank account.

dividend warrant An authorization from an organization for a bank to pay a dividend to a stockholder.

D/N 1. *debit note*. 2. *dispatch note*.

docket 1. A short summary of contents attached to the outside of a packet or document. 2. A Customs house warrant certifying that duty has been paid. 3. (USA) A list of court cases awaiting trial.

document Any specific paper or writing.

document of title A document which provides evidence that the holder has legal ownership of goods.

documentary bill A bill of exchange used as part of a *documentary collection* whereby an exporter sends the bill to the buyer through a bank or banks with certain shipping documents. These will include the invoice, a *document of title* such as a bill of lading and any other documents necessary to effect import to the buyer's country. A bill of exchange not accompanied by documents is called a clean bill of exchange.

documentary credit or **documentary letter of credit** An arrangement whereby a bank in the exporter's country is authorized by the importer or a bank acting on the importer's instructions, to make a payment or accept a bill of exchange on presentation of satisfactory shipping documents showing that the goods have been shipped. Banks will normally require an irrevocable letter of credit so that payment is bound to be made if the terms of the credit are complied with. The most satisfactory arrangement from the exporter's point of view is for the credit to be confirmed by the bank authorized to receive the documents and make the payment. A documentary credit may provide for immediate payment or for the acceptance of a term bill of exchange.

dollar stocks Canadian or US securities.

domicile or domicil The place where a person has his or her true, fixed and permanent home. This is often of considerable significance in deciding liability to personal taxation.

domiciled bill A bill of exchange not made payable at the residence or place of business of the acceptor but one where the place of payment is inserted at the time of acceptance.

door-to-door Transport service from the factory or warehouse of the sender to the address of the consignee.

dormant balance Money in a bank to the credit of a customer in whose account there have been no recent dealings.

dormant partner The equivalent of sleeping partner. See *sleeping partner*.

DOS Disk Operating System. A computer system in which material is stored on disks.

dot matrix printer A computer-operated printer that produces figures and characters by spraying patterns of dots through a grid.

double account system A method of accounts presentation which aims to show the capital raised and the fixed assets on which it has been expended.

double entry accounting An accounting method whereby every transaction is recorded by two entries so that one entry equals the other.

double taxation relief An arrangement between two or more countries to ensure that the same income or profits, etc., are not subject to taxation in more than one country.

doubtful debts provision A charge against profits

in order to to make provisions for possible bad debts.

douceur A *sweetener*, a gratuity for exercising influence or power for the benefit of another.

Dow-Jones Industrial Average An index compiled by Dow Jones and Company, showing movements in the prices of the shares of 30 leading industrial corporations in the USA. Similar to the Financial Times Index in the UK.

downtown (USA) A central business area.

DP Data processing. The manipulation of data by computer operation.

draft 1. A document in a form before its completed state. 2. A written order to pay money, especially one addressed to a bank and the money so paid. 3. A bill of exchange before acceptance.

drawback The sum refunded by government in respect of import duty previously paid on goods re-exported and consequently not liable to duty.

drawee One on whom an instrument of payment, such as a cheque, is drawn.

drawer One drawing up an instrument of payment to be met by another.

drawing rights Original rights of members of the International Monetary Fund to purchase reserves of foreign currency from the Fund. Later supplemented by Special Drawing Rights. See *SDRs*.

drawings account In accounting the account used to record all sums drawn for business use by the proprietor or partners of a business.

drawn bonds Bonds which have been drawn at one of the periodical drawings for payment on a certain date and after which time all interest on them will cease.

drug in the market Goods in such plentiful supply that they are unsaleable.

dry goods In the UK a term applied to tobacco, snuffs, cigars, drugs, dyes, spices, coffee, tea, chicory, cocoa, dried fruits, etc. In the USA the term means drapery goods.

D/S Days' sight, i.e. days after sight (bills of exchange).

dual capacity A stock exchange term referring to the ability of jobber and broker to undertake either of the other's functions in a stock market.

dues 1. Certain charges made by dock and other companies for the temporary use of their property. 2. Advance orders for supply at some future date.

dumping In international trade, selling in a foreign market at a low price subsidized by a higher home price.

dunnage Loose material used in stowing a ship's cargo to protect it from damage during the voyage.

Dutch auction See *auction*.

duties Taxes on merchandise and manufactures, payable either through Customs or Excise, and all other imposts levied by a government.

E

E & OE Errors and omissions excepted.

EE Errors excepted.

earned income A term used in British taxation to refer to income from work, including salaries, wages, profits, and pensions.

earnest or earnest money Money or property given by a purchaser to a seller to bind an oral bargain between them.

earnings rate A firm's net profits divided by its paid-up capital.

easement A right enjoyed by one person over the property of another, such as a right of way (positive), or the right to prevent the other from doing something on or with his or her land (negative).

ECGD Export Credits Guarantee Department. A British government department which encourages exports by providing insurance cover and guarantees for risks that would not normally be available in commercial insurance markets.

Economic Development Committee A sub-committee of the British National Economic Development Council, having the responsibility of examining and advising one particular industry or group of industries.

economic life A term applied to a project or investment to indicate the period of time before the costs of maintenance, upkeep, etc., make it no longer worthwhile to sustain.

economies of scale The observed tendency for the average costs of production to fall either as output is increased or as larger capacity equipment is used.

ECU European Currency Unit. The official unit of account of the European Monetary System.

EDP Electronic data processing. The use of computers for high speed organization, collation and calculation using data fed into the computer.

EEC European Economic Community. See *European Communities* and *European Economic Community*.

EFTA European Free Trade Association.

electronic mail Messages sent from one user of a computer system to one or more recipients using electronic communication and storage techniques. It can combine text, graphics, voice, *facsimile* and other information in a single message. Other functions often performed by an electronic mail system include checking a user's identity, the expansion of named mailing lists into lists of recipients and the interrogation of directories to locate a user from partial information.

electronic office An office environment supported by integrated office automated systems, including word processing, management communications and advanced text management. The office is likely to be linked to other management support, electronic mail and data processing systems.

Electronic Publishing A general term used to describe computer based systems of publishing information in which use is made of telecommunication channels such as the television and telephone services. Examples in the UK include Prestel, Ceefax, Oracle. See also *teletext*.

eligible banks Those banks whose acceptances are eligible for re-discount at the Bank of England. See also *bills of exchange*.

embargo 1. A government order to prevent ships from loading or unloading certain goods or from entering or leaving a port, sometimes enforced in times of war. 2. An authoritative order to prevent the removal of property, pending some judicial proceeding against the owner.

embedded command A command inserted into computer or word processing text in order to set or modify the format in which the text is to be printed. The command is visible on the screen but does not appear in the printed version.

embezzle Dishonestly to turn to one's own use money belonging to, or intended for, one's employer.

employee One who works on a continuous basis for another under a contract of employment, for a wage or salary.

employee participation Provision for employees to have a formal say in the preparation of a firm's programmes and policies and their implementation.

employers' association An organization of employers among whose activities are negotiation with trade unions and the representation of employers' views to official bodies and the public.

employment agency or bureau Organization providing firms with a service by introducing suitable candidates for employment.

Employment Protection Acts UK legislation providing employees with statutory protection against unfair dismissal and with other rights.

end user certificate Written declaration as to the identity of the person who will finally use a product. End user certificates must be provided to obtain UK export licences for military goods.

endorse To transfer by *endorsement* to another, the *transferee*, a document and the rights provided by that document. The person who endorses the document is the *endorser*. Documents commonly transferred by endorsement include bills of exchange, cheques and bills of lading.

endorsement Anything written upon the back of a document, or in a general sense, writing one's name upon the back of a document, such as a cheque, so that the payment can be made to another.

enterprise zone Small geographical area in the UK designated by the British government. These zones offer various relaxations from taxation, planning and other regulations.

entrepôt An intermediate port or warehouse for the temporary reception of goods in transit to another country. Hence *entrepôt trade*, the handling of goods in passage between two other countries.

entrepreneur One who organizes a business and undertakes the risks of enterprise in the anticipation of profit.

entry A document passed to the Customs providing full details of goods for which clearance for import is requested. The precise entry forms used depend on the country of export, the nature of the goods, their liability for duty, if any, and the port of entry. The main ports and airports in the UK have facilities for computer links and the use of computer forms. Similar detailed lists of goods for export are known as *pre-entries*.

Equal Opportunities Commission The body which, in the UK is responsible for applying the law relating to equal opportunities and generally promoting equal opportunities for men and women.

equities Ordinary shares or stock.

equity of redemption The right of the mortgagor to redeem the mortgage on payment of the debt, interest and costs though the stipulated time for payment has passed.

equity share capital The company's issued share capital but excluding any part which carries any right to participate beyond a specified amount in a distribution.

ergonomics The systematic study of work, with the object of finding ways of designing tools, machines and the work environment to make the most efficient use of labour.

escalation clause Clause written into a contract allowing for an increase in the price if the costs of inputs such as labour, fuel or materials, increase.

escalator clause Wage agreement allowing for periodic cost-of-living increases in line with increases in, for example, a retail prices index.

escape clause A clause allowing the release of one or more parties from a contract if certain contingencies arise.

escrow A document, deed, etc., held in escrow has been delivered to an independent person to be held in trust and only released after some duty has been performed.

establishment A business organization, in particular its physical location such as an office, factory, mine or farm.

establishment charge See *overheads*.

estate agent One who acts on behalf of another in the selling, renting, letting of real estate. Same as *realtor* (USA).

estimate An approximate calculation of the charges or cost of an undertaking, given by those who wish to contract for the supply of certain goods, repairs, or other work.

estoppel A legal term which implies that owing to an action or representation made by an individual this person is prevented or 'stopped' from controverting the conclusion that could reasonably be drawn from such words or conduct.

ETA Estimated time of arrival.

ETD Estimated time of departure.

ETS Estimated time of sailing.

Eurocurrency Deposits of currencies held and lent (not necessarily in Europe) outside their countries of origin and outside the control of these countries' monetary authorities. The most important of these are *Eurodollars*, which are dollar deposits held outside the USA and lent to borrowers outside the USA and hence not subject to US monetary regulations. The Eurocurrency market is an important part of the international finance market.

European Assembly Official title of the European Parliament, an assembly directly elected by the voters of the European Communities and with limited powers of review over the European Commission and budget.

European Commission See *Commission of the European Communities*.

European Communities The European Atomic Energy Community, European Coal and Steel Community and European Economic Community which are now integrated and have common institutions. They are still commonly and erroneously referred to as the *EEC* or the *Common Market*.

European Council (of Ministers) The decision-making and policy-forming body of the European Communities. It is formed from the relevant ministers for each policy area from each member state. The term 'European Council' is sometimes reserved for meetings of the heads of governments.

European Court of Justice A European Community institution which is responsible for making legal decisions arising out of the Treaty of Rome on whose provisions the European Community was founded.

European currency unit (ECU) Unit of account fixed in terms of a 'basket' of currencies of member states of the European Communities and used for valuation, budget and debt settlement.

European Economic Community Economic association of European countries with the features of a common market in most goods and some services, free movement of capital and labour, a common agricultural policy, a common tariff for imports from outside the Community and other co-ordinated policies.

European Free Trade Association A trade association providing for free trade in industrial goods between a number of European countries which are not members of the European Communities.

European Monetary System (EMS) A structure for currency co-operation between members of the Community whereby the currency exchange rates of the majority of members are linked together.

European Parliament The name by which the European Assembly affects to be known. Members style themselves as MEP (Member of the European Parliament).

even On the stock exchange, when securities are carried over 'at even' there is neither *backwardation* nor *contango* to pay.

ex 1. Without. Contrast *cum*. Hence: *ex all*, without dividend, bonus or return of capital and without rights to any new stocks or shares about to be issued; *ex coupon*, without the interest coupon; *ex div or ex dividend*, without accrued dividend; *ex interest*, without accrued interest; *ex new*, without any right to claim new stock or shares about to be issued. 2. Out of or from. Hence: *ex gratia payment* (payment out of grace), a payment made without legal liability to do so; *ex officio*, by virtue of office; *ex quay*, an international price term signifying that the buyer is responsible for all costs (including duty unless stated 'duty paid') from the time the goods arrive at the quay (wharf) of destination; *ex ship*, an international price term signifying that the seller bears all costs of getting the goods to the destination on board the ship but all further costs, including unloading are paid by the buyer; *ex stock*, from existing stock as opposed to future production; *ex works (ex factory, ex mill, ex warehouse*, etc.), an international price term indicating that all costs and risks of transport from the seller's premises are the responsibility of the buyer.

excess In motor insurance claims, that first part for which the policyholder is responsible. The insurance policy covers the balance above the amount of any agreed excess.

exchange 1. A place where merchants and dealers meet to transact business. 2. The transfer of one thing in return for another and hence the discharge of a debt without payment of money brought about by a *bill of exchange*.

exchange control Any system whereby the movement of currency across national frontiers is regulated and restricted.

exchange equalization fund Account at the Bank of England, controlled by the Treasury, and used to purchase and sell sterling and foreign exchange in order to influence exchange rates.

exchange rate Price of one currency in terms of another.

excise An inland tax imposed at the point of manufacture of certain goods, mostly alcohol and tobacco.

executive A manager with significant decision

making and administrative responsibilities in an organization.

executor One chosen by the testator (person making a will) to carry out the provisions of the will. A female executor is termed an *executrix*. Contrast *administrator*.

exotic currency A currency for which there is little demand for purposes of international trade and which is not widely traded on foreign exchanges.

expected to rank In bankruptcy those debts likely to be proved and so to qualify for a share in any dividend.

exports Goods and services sold by *exporters* to foreign buyers for use in foreign countries.

express international money transfer A system used in international trade whereby money is transferred by coded inter-bank telex. See *telegraphic transfer*.

extraordinary resolution In company law a resolution passed by a three-quarters majority at a general meeting conforming to certain statutory rules. Contrast *ordinary resolution*.

F

FAA Free of all average. A term used in marine insurance. See *average (2)*.

face value The nominal value of bonds, stocks, shares, certificates, etc. The amount, before discount or premium is taken into account, of issue, as opposed to their market value which may be higher or lower.

facsimile transmission A system that provides transmission by electronic signals of ordinary documents, including drawings, photographs and maps.

factor 1. An agent who sells goods or services on behalf of a principal but who deals in his own name and has the goods in his possession. 2. One who provides the services of *factoring debts*, that is collecting and guaranteeing the payment of customers debts to and on behalf of clients. Much of the administration and the risks of debt collection pass to the factor.

factor comparison job evaluation A system of assigning jobs to particular pay scales through an examination of the different factors of skill, experience, responsibility, etc., required to perform the job.

factor of production Traditionally in economics, one of the basic elements in the production process, these being identified as *capital*, *labour*, *land* and sometimes enterprise. Recently the term has been used to mean any good or service used in a production process.

failure to agree Formal recognition of a breakdown in management-worker negotiations.

Fair Labor Standards Act (USA) Federal law governing wages and hours of work in industries producing goods for commerce.

fair trade System of international trade in which countries allow similar conditions to importers as their exporters in turn receive.

FAS Free alongside ship. An international price term indicating that the seller is responsible for all costs up to placing the goods alongside the ship. Further costs and risks, including loading on to the ship and clearing the goods for export are the responsibility of the buyer.

fast food Quickly cooked food sold in eatable form and with a minimum of waiting time on the part of the customer. It may be eaten on or off the premises.

FCO Franco confine. A price term with the same meaning as *delivered at frontier*.

feasibility study A study carried out prior to a development project to establish that the proposed system is feasible and can serve a useful purpose. A study can be a paper exercise or include the construction of a prototype.

Federal Reserve System (USA) Twelve local Federal Reserve Banks under the central control of the Federal Reserve Board, together acting as the *central bank* of the USA.

Federal Trade Commission (USA) Agency responsible for the enforcement of antitrust laws and prevention of unfair competition.

FGA Free of general average. A term used in marine insurance. See *average (2)*.

fiat Formal command. A short order or warrant of some judge or public officer for making out and allowing certain processes.

fibre optics transmission system A data communications system that uses *optical fibres* instead of copper wire. The information is carried by modulating light. A transmission cable consists of large bundles of these small lightweight nonconductive fibres.

fictitious assets Those items which appear as assets in a balance sheet but which do not represent value that can be realized, e.g. preliminary expenses not written off.

fictitious payee A payee named on a cheque or bill of exchange who does not exist. The effect is to make the cheque, etc., payable to bearer.

fidelity guarantee A guarantee by which a surety (often an insurance office) is responsible for the honesty of a person employed in a particular office or vocation.

fiduciary issue Notes and coin issued by the central bank of the country and backed by no cover other than that government's securities.

fiduciary loan A loan granted without security upon the confidence of the honour of the borrower.

field In computing, a component of a record corresponding to one item of data. Field size or width is often used to indicate the extent of the item of data for input, storage and output operations. The 'name' field on a record may have a field of 20 characters, for example.

FIFO First in, first out. A system of costing materials and stocks used in production on the assumption that the first into stores are the first to be subsequently used. Contrast *LIFO*.

file 1. A collection of papers, documents etc., relating to a particular topic or person. 2. An identifiable quantity of data stored in computer system.

final dividend The last instalment of the dividend paid by a limited company in respect of any one financial year.

finance The raising and provision of money for public or commercial undertakings. The money so provided.

Finance Act The Act of Parliament giving effect to a Budget of the British government.

finance company A firm whose major business is the financing of hire purchase and similar instalment credit arrangements.

finance house A term commonly used in the UK for a *finance company*.

financial accounting The systematic recording in monetary terms of information about a firm, primarily for people such as creditors, shareholders and tax authorities, other than the firm's managers. Compare *cost accounting* and *management accounting*.

financial institution A general term often used to refer to the banks, insurance offices, pension funds and other institutions which have substantial funds available for investment and which manage investments on behalf of clients.

financial ratio One of a number of ratios between two items in an organization's accounts used for the analysis of performance.

Financial Times Indexes (or Indices) Indexes, published in the *Financial Times* newspaper, showing movements in the prices of British securities. The most widely known is the FT Industrial Ordinary Share Index which is based on the share prices of 30 leading shares held to be representative of the market as a whole. This index is sometimes simply referred to as the 'FT Index'.

financial year An accounting period. In the UK it is defined by the Companies Acts as the period covered by a company's accounts. This period may be more or less than a calendar year.

financier One who raises or supplies capital for

undertakings or who manages the finances of an organization.

fine paper The same as *first class paper*.

FIO Free in and out. A price term indicating that the seller is responsible for all charges up to the point where goods are off loaded on to the quay at the port of destination. The buyer is responsible for all further cost, including stevedore charges.

firm A general term for an organization of people or a sole proprietor, producing goods or services for sale to others.

firm offer A definite offer to purchase specified property at a given price.

firmware A computing term meaning *programs* stored permanently in the computer system in such a way that they cannot be modified or erased. Such programs are typically built into microcomputers in the factory.

first class paper A term used in the money market to refer to bills of exchange, promissory notes and similar instruments which are backed by well known banks or leading financial institutions, especially those eligible for re-discounting by the Bank of England. The British government's own treasury bills and bonds would be included in this term.

first day premium The amount by which shares rise above their issue price in the first day of dealing on a stock exchange.

FIS Free into store. A price term used in relation to trade with certain countries including the Baltic countries. It indicates that the seller is responsible for all charges up to delivery at a designated store in the country of destination.

fiscal period (USA) Equivalent of UK *accounting period*.

fiscal year 1. The government's own financial year and the period used for assessing liability to taxation. In the UK this year ends on April 5th. 2. (USA) The accounting year.

fixed assets Long lasting assets such as plant and machinery, which are acquired to assist the production process and are neither intended for resale nor for rapid absorption in the production process.

fixed capital The same as *fixed assets*.

fixed charges An accounting term for those charges which recur regularly regardless of the business transacted. They include rent or property taxes. Mortgage debentures are said to represent a 'fixed charge' on certain of the undertaking's immovable assets such as land or buildings.

fixed cost A cost of production that does not vary directly as the level of production changes within certain output or turnover limits. It is also known as *period cost*.

flag discrimination Preferential treatment in relation to charges and facilities to the ships of one nation over others.

flags of convenience The national flags of certain countries that are prepared to register ships owned by nationals of other countries and which offer the ship owners advantages in terms of taxation, registration and standards, etc.

float 1. To start a company, producing the initial capital and making initial arrangements. 2. An initial amount of cash.

floating assets The same as *current assets*.

floating capital Money or assets that can quickly be converted to money, available for meeting the expenses of operating a concern.

floating charge A mortgage or charge given by the debentures of a company to cover the circulating assets, e.g. stock in trade and book debts.

floating debt A debt which may be called for repayment at short notice.

floating mortgage A security or charge which affects a variety of assets and may attach to any one class leaving the others unaffected.

floating policy An insurance term for a policy which covers moveable goods, equipment, etc., which may be in any one of a number of areas.

floor to floor time A term, especially in engineering, indicating the period between picking up a component and depositing it after an operation or process on it has been completed.

floppy disk A lightweight flexible computer disk

which behaves as if it were rigid when rotating at speed.

flow chart A graphic representation of the major steps of a work process.

FOB Free on board. An international price term indicating that the seller is responsible for all costs up to and including placing the goods on to the ship. Further costs, including freight, are the liability of the buyer.

FOB airport An international price term which is always followed by a named airport. It does not have the literal meaning of the shipping term *FOB* but indicates that the seller's responsibility ceases when goods have been delivered to the care of an agreed air carrier at the designated airport. Further risks and costs are the responsibility of the buyer.

FOC 1. Father of the Chapel. The equivalent of *shop steward* in certain trade unions. 2. Fire Offices Committee. A group of leading British fire insurance offices with the function of reducing fire hazards, encouraging sound fire protection practices and promoting insurance procedures and charges likely to promote these aims.

folio The number of a page in a bookkeeping journal or of two pages facing each other.

FOR/FOT Free on rail/free on truck. An international price term used only when goods are to be carried by rail and stating the rail departure point. It indicates that the seller is responsible for all costs up to loading the goods on to the rail truck (if a full load) or, in the case of a part wagon load, into the care of the railway company. Further costs and risks are the liability of the buyer.

for money A stock exchange term for transactions paid for at the time they are made.

for the account A stock exchange term for transactions to be settled on at the next *settlement day*.

force majeure Events beyond the control of the parties to a contract, e.g. actions of war, strikes or natural disasters, and which release them from the contract.

foreclose To take possession of estate or other things mortgaged with a view to repaying the loan.

foredate To date before true time.

foreign bills of exchange Bills drawn in one country and made payable in another.

foreign exchange Foreign currency.

foreman One in charge of a group of workers.

forfaiting The practice whereby an exporter obtains a cash advance from a financial institution on the security of goods contracted for export. The term is derived from French *forfait*, surrender of rights to something.

form letter A stock letter used when the same information is to be sent to numbers of different people.

format The defined structure of the pattern of information that is recorded on magnetic media, displayed on a visual display unit or printed on paper.

FORTRAN From Formula Translation. A computer language, based on English and algebraic expressions, widely used for scientific and mathematical purposes.

forward 1. A term used of contracts, etc., for delivery at some date in the future. Examples include: *forward contract*, a contract for delivery at a future date; *forward exchange*, purchase of foreign currency for delivery at a future date; *forward price*, the price quoted in forward contracts; *forward rate*, the rate quoted for forward exchange contracts. 2. To arrange the collection, dispatch and delivery of goods. This work is often undertaken by *forwarding agents*.

founders' shares Company shares granted to the founders of a company in consideration of their efforts, costs and risks in carrying through the flotation. They usually carry valuable voting rights and rights to profits after the ordinary shareholders have received a dividend. They are disliked by stock exchanges and financial institutions because they reduce the rights of the ordinary shareholders.

franchise 1. An exclusive right to manufacture, sell or distribute the goods or services of another in a designated area. 2. An amount of loss in marine insurance which is carried by the cargo-owner, the insurer bearing losses over this amount. The object is to discourage small claims.

franco Free, used in the French version of the international price terms: *franco bord* (see *FOB*); *franco le long du navire* (see *FAS*; *franco transporteur* (see *free carrier*) and *franco wagon* (see *FOR/FOT*).

franked investment income In the UK, investment income on which tax (advance corporation tax) has already been paid.

fraudulent preference A transfer of property or any payment made by a person unable to meet debts when due, in favour of a creditor with a view to giving such creditor a preference over others.

free carrier An international price term used with a named point or range of points and intended for use when 'multimodal' methods of transport are used, e.g. when containers are carried by road, rail and ship. The seller's responsibilities for costs end when the goods have been delivered to the care of the carrier at the stated point or range of agreed points.

free enterprise Production for profit of goods and services by private individuals and companies without government subsidy or participation.

free house A public house or other licensed establishment that is not tied to, i.e. not bound to purchase exclusively from, a particular brewer.

free of particular average Goods specified in this way

under a marine insurance contract are covered only in the event of a 'total loss' to the ship and cargo. Such goods are usually especially vulnerable to damage during transportation.

free trade International trade without the impediment of tariffs, quotas or other artificial restrictions.

freehold In the UK the right to hold and dispose of land with almost the full legal rights of ownership. It is the highest form of ownership of land possible in the UK.

freeport A port or other designated area where goods may be received from a foreign country, worked on or prepared for distribution and then re-exported without payment of import or export duties.

freight 1. Goods transported by sea or air and in the USA, by road and rail. 2. The charges made for carrying such goods. 3. The profit made by shipowners on the carriage of such goods.

freight/carriage paid to... An international price term indicating that the seller's responsibilities end, and the buyer's commence, when the goods have been delivered to the care of the carrier at a stated destination.

freight/carriage and insurance paid to... An international price term meaning the same as *freight/carriage paid to...* but, in addition, insurance arrangements, as agreed between the parties, are made and paid for by the seller.

freight forward A term used to indicate that freight is payable at the port of destination.

freight notes Statements sent out by shipbrokers to shippers of goods showing the amount due for freight on goods shipped.

freight release A document or bill of lading endorsement by shipbrokers confirming that 'freight forward' has been paid and authorizing the release of goods.

freighter 1. A ship or aircraft that primarily carries goods. 2. The charterer of a ship or aircraft.

friendly society In the UK, a non-profit-making organization, maintained from members' subscriptions, and primarily concerned with providing various benefits such as loans and insurance to members.

fringe benefit A reward paid to employees other than as monetary wages or salary. It can include the use of a company owned car, pension rights or a health care scheme.

frozen assets, credit, funds, etc. Assets, etc., to which access is denied and which cannot be moved or transferred.

frustration of contract The ending of the duties of parties to a contract due to circumstances unforeseen at the time of making the contact and which now make it impossible to discharge.

full cost pricing A system of pricing designed to ensure that the sales revenue will be sufficient to cover all direct costs plus an appropriate contribution to indirect costs and profits.

functional department A department of a business responsible for an activity, such as purchasing, marketing or transport, relating to one or a range of products.

functional organization A system of organization in which each specific function, common to all or several departments, is in the hands of one person throughout.

funded or permanent debts The debt which the government is not under an obligation to pay at any fixed time. In the UK such debt is represented by *consols*.

funds 1. Stock or capital. 2. Money, the income of which is set apart for some permanent object. 3. Government stock and public securities.

futures contracts Contracts for the delivery of goods at a fixed future date, at a fixed price, these contracts are usually used for *hedging* against uncertainty and only a small proportion of such contracts actually result in the delivery of goods. Futures contracts may be bought and sold in futures markets

G

Gantt chart Chart using standard symbols showing the relationship between planned and actual performance. After H.L. Gantt, an American industrial engineer.

garnishee A third party who owes money to, or holds the goods of, another who is a judgment debtor.

garnishee order An order served on persons owing a judgment debtor money, warning them not to part with such money pending a settlement of the claim against the debtor. The object is to prevent the debtor receiving the money and applying it to any purpose other than paying the creditors.

garnishment The notice given to garnishees, in cases of attachment, warning them not to part with money or goods in their possession, pending the settlement of some claim against the owner.

GATT An international agreement, now having over 80 member nations, to work to encourage greater multinational trade through a series of tariff reductions and the removal of quotas and similar obstructions.

Gazette The London Gazette, a publication of the British government, giving official information such as lists of appointments, current state and legal notices and summaries of bankruptcy cases.

GDP Gross domestic product. See *gross domestic product*.

gearing The relationship between the borrowings and the equity capital of a firm. The greater the proportion of borrowings the higher the gearing; the lower the proportion of borrowings, the lower the gearing. See also *leverage*.

general acceptance An accepted bill without special conditions, signifying an unqualified assent to the drawer's order to pay.

general average A proportionate contribution levied on the owners of ship and cargo according to value, to indemnify those who have suffered a loss when a part of the cargo or vessel has been voluntarily sacrificed in order to preserve as much as possible of the venture.

general meeting A meeting that may be attended by all the members of an organization, e.g. by all the shareholders of a company.

general partner See *partners*.

general union A trade union which accepts members drawn from a number of occupations and industries, often including skilled and unskilled workers.

gift inter vivos An unconditional gift of property made prior to death.

gilt-edged security A security of the highest class, e.g. British government stock.

gilts British government securities.

giro A system of making payments to third parties by credit transfer. In the UK a 'bank giro' system is operated for credit transfers between account holders of the various clearing banks. The State owned National Girobank transacts much of its day-to-day business through the Post Office.

give on To pay contango.

glut An excess, in the market, of supply over what can be sold at current market prices.

GNP Gross national product. See *gross national product*.

go slow Action in a labour dispute having much the same effect as *work to rule*.

going concern A firm that is trading and is likely to be able to continue to trade without becoming insolvent. The value of such a firm will reflect its earning power and this value is likely to exceed its *break-up value*, the difference being attributed to *goodwill*.

good merchantable quality and condition A phrase used in making contracts. It means that the goods supplied must be up to the ordinary standard of quality and in their customary sound state.

goodwill An advantage of an established firm over new firms in terms of the likelihood of repeat business from its customers. See also *going concern*.

goods received note Document prepared on receipt of deliveries and subsequently used for stock control purposes.

goods returned note Similar to a *goods received note* but prepared when a firm's own goods are returned to it.

graphics A term used in computing to denote a mode of computer processing and output in which a significant part of the information is presented in pictorial form. The presentation may be on a screen or on paper and may include graphs and other forms of statistical illustration.

graphics tablet A computer input device where the movement of a pen of a sensitive pad is translated into signals which give the pen's position.

grievance procedure An established series of stages through which attempts are made to resolve a dispute between a worker or workers and the employer.

gross The full amount or weight of anything before having made any allowance or deduction. Hence, for example: *gross income*, income from all sources, without any deduction of expenses or taxation; *gross profit*, the difference between sales revenue and direct costs of production without deduction of indirect costs; *gross receipts*, the total receipts before any deduction is made for expenses.

gross domestic product The total value of goods and services produced within a country in a specified time period. It exceeds *net domestic product* by the amount of capital depreciation in the period.

gross national product Total value of goods and services produced by the residents of a country in a specified time period. Unlike *GDP* it excludes the earnings of foreign residents within the country but includes the income of residents from property held abroad.

gross weight The combined weight of both goods and packing. The weight of the package in which goods are enclosed is called, in the UK, the *tare* and the weight of the goods themselves, the *net* weight.

ground rent The rent paid to a landlord for the freedom to build on or use the land.

group income For UK corporation tax purposes, dividends paid by one of a 'group of companies' to another within the group in accordance with arrangements agreed within the group are not subject to advance corporation tax as far as the former company is concerned. At the same time the receiving company does not have any tax credit from the dividend payments.

group insurance Insurance of a group of people under a single policy, especially in life or accident insurance.

groupage Combining several consignments of goods into a single load for one container. Hence a *groupage depot*, a place where groupage is undertaken.

guarantee (USA often **guaranty**) 1. A conditional or secondary responsibility taken by a person, called a *guarantor* on another's account, whereby he undertakes to fulfil certain engagements such as the payment of money, in the event of the other's failure to meet a liability to do so. 2. A promise given by a producer to remedy defects in goods sold should any appear within a given time period.

guarantee company A company *limited by guarantee*.

guarantee fund A fund formed by regularly setting aside a portion of the profits to meet any exceptional losses.

guarantee insurance Insurance to cover the failure of a third party to discharge an obligation to the insured.

guaranteed bonds A bond issued by one company where the payment of which is guaranteed by another.

guaranteed stock Stock issued by a company where the payment of dividends is guaranteed by another body such as the government.

guaranteed (working) week The minimum amount of time for which a firm undertakes to pay a worker as long as that worker is available for work, regardless of the time actually worked.

guild A society or body of individuals formed to promote the interests of the particular trade or calling to which the members belong.

H

hacker A programmer with an obsessive interest in tinkering with computer systems, usually with the purpose of matching his or her skill against those of the systems designer. The term has become widely known in relation to those who achieve access to systems to which they have no right of access. Some are tempted to use their skills to create mischief or to pursue criminal purposes.

Hague rules The rules governing rights and liabilities of ships and carriers at sea and which have their origins in a conference at The Hague in 1921.

half-commission man Stock exchange term for one who is not a stock exchange member but who introduces business for a half share in the commission.

hall mark An official mark affixed to jewellery, plate and other articles made of gold or silver to serve as a proof that they have been tested and found to be of legal quality and of the fineness stamped on them.

handsel Earnest money. Money paid to bind a bargain.

harbour dues Sums paid by ships for entering harbour and the use of certain harbour facilities.

hard copy A printed or otherwise permanent copy of data from a processing system.

hard disk A rigid magnetic computer disk. It normally allows a higher recording density than a *floppy disk* to provide more storage for the same physical dimensions.

hardware The physical equipment required to form and operate a computer.

haulage 1. Movement of heavy or bulky goods by road, rail or canal. 2. Charges made for such transport, exclusive of loading and unloading.

head lease A lease granted by a freeholder to the first leaseholder who may then subsequently assign the diminishing term to others.

hedging Operation on a *futures market* to insure against losses caused by fluctuations in price. For example, a manufacturer may buy futures to ensure a guaranteed price of raw materials and sell futures to guarantee a price for the product.

heriditable bond A bond having a conveyance of land attached to it and given as a security for the faithful repayment of money lent or owing, the latter documents being available in the event of the bond not being honoured or the interest not paid when due.

HGV Heavy goods vehicle. In the UK this is broadly defined as an articulated goods vehicle or a large goods vehicle constructed or adapted to carry or haul goods and with a permissible maximum weight, including trailer, exceeding 7.5 tonnes.

hidden reserve A secret reserve, not disclosed in the

accounts. It may be created by the undervaluation of assets such as stocks, or the overvaluation of liabilities such as provisions for claims in the case of an insurance company.

high level language A type of computer programming language in which the instructions reflect the requirements of the programmer rather than the facilities and method of operations provided by the computer *hardware*.

high seas The open sea beyond the territorial waters and hence beyond the control of any nation.

hire 1. Wages paid or service. 2. The price paid for the temporary use of any article.

hire purchase A system of purchase in instalments. Strictly, until the final instalment is paid, the goods are only hired and title does not pass to the buyer but under British law the rights of the legal owner to recover the goods are strictly limited once a certain proportion of the total purchase price has been paid.

histogram A statistical illustration in which the values or proportions of a variable element are represented by bars or divisions within a bar.

historic cost For accounting purposes the cost of something recorded as the actual money paid at some past date. This may be very different from the real current value because of the effects of inflation or the appreciation of an asset.

holder In relation to bills of exchange the holder is

one who has possession of a bill either directly or by transfer. One who holds a bill for which value has been given at some stage in its history is a *holder for value* as regards prior parties to the bill. A holder who has a lien on a bill is a holder for value to the extent of the lien. A *holder in due course* is one who has taken in good faith and for value, a bill, complete and regular on the face of it and who became the owner before it was overdue and without any notice of previous dishonour or defect in the title of the person who negotiates it.

holding company 1. A company that holds more than 50 per cent of the nominal value of the equity share capital of another company or is a member of another company and controls the composition of its board of directors. Contrast *subsidiary company*. 2. A company whose primary business lies in holding the shares of other firms.

holding deed The deed which conveys the ownership of freehold land to the present owner.

home consumption Of a country, includes the goods and services actually consumed in that country, whether produced at home or imported.

home trade 1. Trade in goods and services in the domestic market as opposed to exports. 2. In UK shipping parlance, shipping between ports in the British Isles, and some nearby ports in the continent of Europe.

home value declaration A declaration of the value of goods carried in the country of origin at the date of the invoice.

honorarium A voluntary fee paid in recognition of services, especially professional services.

honorary Holding a title or office without receiving a fee or salary.

honour (USA honor) To accept and meet some claim or obligation; for example to honour a cheque means to pay the amount for which the cheque is drawn.

horizontal combination or **horizontal integration** or **horizontal merger** A combination of two or more firms mainly operating in the same industry and at the same stage of the production chain. For example, the amalgamation of two microcomputer manufacturers. Contrast *vertical combination*.

house A name sometimes applied to a business organization, especially one concerned with finance, distribution or international trade. The 'House' means one or other of: the Bankers' Clearing House, The London Stock Exchange, the House of Commons or Christ Church, University of Oxford. *In house* refers to an activity carried out by the organization's own employees as opposed to work contracted out to other firms.

house advertising Advertising with the object of publicising or improving the public image of the firm as opposed to specific products of the firm.

house magazine Journal published by a business for circulation among its own members and employees.

house union A trade union whose membership is confined to employees of a single firm.

hypothec In Scottish law, a security in favour of a creditor over the property of the debtor while the property remains in the possession of the debtor.

hypothecate To place or assign property as security under an agreement; to pledge or mortgage.

hypothecation Giving lien upon property or pledging documents which convey a right to property – mortgages, bottomry bonds, bills of sale etc – but still retaining possession of the property pledged. Some foreign governments may issue bonds, pledging certain of the customs, revenues, duties or taxes as security for a public loan. In such cases of hypothecation, certain rights are made over which are not yet collected or not yet in existence.

I

IATA International Air Transport Association. A group of over 50 major air lines which negotiate together for the allocation of air routes.

IBRD International Bank for Reconstruction and Development. A member of the World Bank Group and often referred to as the World Bank. Its main function is to provide a channel for finance and knowledge for the development of the lesser developed countries of the world.

ICD Inland clearance depot. A Customs approved place to which goods imported in containers may be taken for entry examination and clearance, also where any goods intended for export in containers may be inspected, locked and sealed.

ICFC Industrial and Commercial Finance Corporation. A British financial institution formed to assist in the financing and development of small businesses. It is now a division of Investors for Industry plc.

IFC International Finance Corporation. Part of the World Bank Group.

IMF International Monetary Fund. Originally established after the Bretton Woods Conference in 1944 with the object of stabilizing the exchange rate system between countries and assisting countries with balance of payments problems.

immediate access store Part of a computer's memory to which access can be gained immediately regardless of any previous access.

impersonal accounts An accounting term for accounts concerned with things other than people, e.g. *real* or *property* accounts such as cash, plant or goods, and *nominal* accounts, such as rent, rates or discounts.

import duties Taxes imposed on goods entering the country.

import licence Document issued by a government authorizing the import of goods.

import quota The specified quantity of a particular class of goods that a government will permit to be imported or imported from a certain country.

imports A collective term for all the goods, commodities and services produced in another country but brought into the home country for consumption.

imposts Taxes, especially those on imports.

impressed stamps The stamp duty on certain documents is payable by an impressed stamp. The document is taken to the stamping office and, on payment of duty, the stamp is impressed into the document.

imprest system The method by which a fixed amount is advanced and the expenditure from that amount is made good at regular intervals so that there is a constant balance at the end of each interval.

impulse buying Purchases made by customers as the result of a sudden decision, usually on seeing the goods at the place of sale. An unplanned purchase.

impute To place an estimated value upon. For example, an imputed rent may be estimated for property actually owned by a firm to show the rent it would have to pay to a landlord or which could be earned by letting to another. This is a method of taking into account the real or *opportunity cost* of using the firm's own property.

in bond Goods are said to be in bond when they are held in a *bonded warehouse* pending payment of duty.

inc Incorporated (USA) Term placed after the name of a company to indicate that it is a legal corporation with limited liability. See *ltd* and *plc*.

income Gain, interest or revenue resulting from employment, business activity or other source.

income and expenditure account An account of a non-profit-seeking but property owning organization and which corresponds to the profit and loss account of a profit-seeking, trading organization. The final balance is the 'excess of income over expenditure', or vice versa, rather than the 'net profit' or 'net loss'. These accounts are usual for clubs, associations and charities.

income statement (USA) The equivalent of the UK *profit and loss account*.

income tax A tax on income.

incorporate To form and register a company under the UK Companies Acts.

incoterms A set of standard price terms and their interpretations as used in international trade, drawn up by the International Chamber of Commerce.

indemnity Financial compensation to make good a loss sustained.

indent An order received from a buyer abroad for specified goods to be purchased on the buyer's behalf. A *closed indent* is one where the foreign buyer specifies the supplier and so leaves nothing to the discretion of the home merchant. An *open indent* is one where the choice of supplier is left to the discretion of the merchant.

indenture A legal document, originally written in duplicate on the same piece of paper with the two copies torn roughly apart in order to prevent forgery. Now a term used particularly of: 1. an apprenticeship agreement; 2. (USA) a contract by a corporation with a trustee for bondholders for the issue of bonds.

index (plural indexes or indices) Numbers that are altered over time to reflect the change in a particular value or set of values. For example, indexes of production, earnings or prices.

Index of Retail Prices The index which, in the UK, is the official monthly index of changes in the prices of certain goods and services which represent typical expenditure patterns. See *cost of living index*.

indirect cost Overhead costs associated with the production of one or more goods and services.

indirect tax A tax collected other than from those who eventually pay it. For example, *value added tax* is eventually paid by the final customers but it is actually collected and paid to the tax authorities by producers. Contrast *direct tax*.

indorse See *endorse*.

industrial relations Relations between employers and their employees or, in practice, between senior managers and trade unions.

Industrial Society, The An association of industrial and commercial companies, employers' associations, public corporations and trade unions having the object of providing training and assistance in the areas of industrial relations and personnel management.

industrial training boards Boards established by the British government and financed by a levy on firms in an industry and having the responsibility for organizing, supervising and promoting training within a particular industry.

industrial tribunals In the UK, tribunals with legal, employers' and trade union representatives that have jurisdiction over disputes arising from various pieces of legislation, covering matters such as *unfair dismissal* and *redundancy*.

industrial union A trade union whose members are drawn from a single industry.

inertia selling The delivery of unsolicited goods to customers on a sale-or-return basis followed by demands for payment. The practice is illegal or subject to strict controls in many countries.

infant One under the age of legal maturity and who is, therefore, restricted in powers to enter into legally binding contracts.

inflation A general and sustained tendency for the level of prices to increase throughout an economy.

information In computing, this relates to collections of symbols which subsequently form patterns that carry meaning to the observer. Such patterns can be created in a number of ways, including: light, sound or radio waves; electric current or voltage; magnetic fields; marks on paper.

information technology The study, development and application of communication systems in relation to such areas of technology as computers, telecommunications, consumer electronics and television and radio broadcasting.

ingot A bar of metal. For non-precious metals ingots are always a preparation for a subsequent production process.

initialize In computing, to prepare a blank disk to receive information.

inherent vice Some peculiarity of goods carried that makes them especially susceptible to loss or damage. Losses due to inherent vice are not covered by marine or transit insurance.

injunction An order of the court commanding something to be done (mandatory injunction) or forbidding some activity (prohibitory injunction).

inland bill A bill of exchange drawn and made payable within a single country.

insider dealing Unfair use of special knowledge of a company's affairs by a director or senior executive to make advantageous bargains on the stock exchange. This practice is either illegal or strictly controlled in most countries.

insolvent The state of being unable to pay the whole of one's debts in full when these are due to be paid.

instalment When a debt is divided into several parts to be paid at intervals, each part is said to be an instalment.

insurable interest A financial interest in some thing or person insured. It is a general legal principle of insurance that there must be a risk of financial loss arising out of the event insured against for legal insurance to be possible. Without such a risk insurance could simply be a form of gambling.

insurance or assurance A contract between two parties, in which one, the *insurer*, in return for a consideration, the *premium*, undertakes to indemnify or insure the other, the *insured*, against certain losses resulting from some specified event or contingency which is often known as the *risk*.

The term assurance is usually applied to insurances arranged on the lives of persons.

insurance broker One who acts as an agent to arrange insurances for another.

insurance certificate A document issued by an insurer to an insured, certifying that certain types of insurance have been effected. Certificates are required by statute in some countries, including the UK, for motor and employers' liability insurance. In marine insurance practice the certificate often represents the policy and can be an important, transferable, shipping document needed in the event of a claim.

insurance policy The written contract of insurance.

intangible asset Any asset that does not possess a physical identity, e.g. *goodwill*.

intelpost The British Royal Mail *facsimile transmission* service.

integrated circuit In computing and electronics, a solid state circuit in which all the components are formed upon a single piece of *semiconductor*.

integrated office automation Electronic office components which have been combined to provide linked, coherent information technology facilities.

interactive system A computer system where there is a response to user instructions as soon as they are entered.

interbank loan Loan, for a fixed period, from one bank to another.

interest 1. See insurable interest. 2. Any share in, or other benefits to be derived from property, business or other undertaking. The parties are said to have an interest in the concern from which they derive a benefit. 3. Money earned as the reward for lending capital to another.

interface A common boundary between two computer systems, devices or programs.

interim dividend A provisional distribution made before the actual dividend is due or before the whole of the profits to be divided have been ascertained.

intermediary One who acts as a go-between between two parties in a business transaction.

internal rate of return That rate of discount which produces a *net present value* for investment of zero. It is often looked on as representing the *rate of return* to the organization of a proposed investment project.

International Monetary Fund See *IMF*.

international union (USA) A union with members from countries other than the USA, e.g. Mexico, Canada.

intestate A person who has died without making a valid will, or leaving property not disposed of in a will, is said to have died intestate.

intra vires Within the powers (of the organization). Contrast *ultra vires*.

inventories (USA) Stocks.

inventory 1. A list of goods etc., intended for sale. 2. A list of household goods and effects kept for reference or for checking between tenant and owner.

investment The giving up of present benefits, such as cash, in order to obtain property, assets, securities, etc., in the expectation of a future gain or income from these. The incurring of a liability, e.g. borrowing money, in the same expectation.

investment appraisal The analysis of possible investment projects as an aid to managerial decisions relating to investment. See *capital budgeting*.

investment bank (USA) An organization which buys the entire new issue of shares by a company and then sells the shares to others in smaller lots. It also undertakes other financial activities on behalf of firms in a manner similar to that of *merchant banking* in the UK.

investment trust A company formed for the purpose of holding, usually long-term, investments.

invisibles Services provided by residents of one country for that of another. They include insurance, banking, merchanting and tourism and transfers and payments out of current income.

invoice A document sent by a seller to a buyer

specifying full material details of the sale and its price, including, where relevant, *VAT*.

IOU A memorandum, signed by a debtor, acknowledging a debt and specifying the amount and date.

IRD Inland rail depot.

irredeemable Not redeemable, so that the issuer of an irredeemable security has no right to require the holder to surrender it nor can the holder require the issuer to redeem it.

irrevocable credit See *documentary credit*.

ISBN International Standard Book Number.

issue price The price at which a security is sold by the issuer.

issued capital That part of the nominal or authorized capital of a company registered in the UK, which has been issued to shareholders.

issuing bank The bank in the importer's country which issues the shipping documents in return for payment or acceptance of a bill of exchange under a documentary credit arrangement.

issuing house An organization whose main activity lies in arranging the public issue of shares, usually in the same way as an *investment bank* in the USA.

IT Information technology.

J

Jason clause Clause, especially in USA contracts, defining the precise terms under which goods are carried.

jerque note A certificate issued to the master of a ship by a Customs officer known as a *jerquer* when the officer has examined and passed the ship's cargo.

job analysis The systematic investigation of a job prior to preparation of a *job description*.

job card The card on which is entered a record of the time spent on any particular operation or job. In addition the job card may contain details of the operations performed.

job description A statement of the work required of an employee in the performance of a particular job.

job design The process of choosing the methods, tasks and responsibilities that are to constitute a particular job.

job enlargement Providing extra tasks and responsibilities for an employee in order to make the work more interesting.

job enrichment Changing the features, other than pay, working conditions or the job itself, of the content of a job in order to increase the satisfaction achieved by the person performing it.

job evaluation Estimating the qualities required for different jobs and their value in the organization, rather than the worth of the employees. For example, estimates are made of the training and experience required, the responsibilities involved and their importance relative to other jobs to the organization.

job number The identification number and/or symbol allotted to each job for, (a) tracing and location purposes, (b) costing.

job rate A pre-arranged basis of payment for the accomplishment of a specified task.

job specification A statement similar to a job description but also detailing the skills, qualifications, experience and other qualities required for the person who will perform the job.

jobbers Those who deal in stocks and shares within a stock exchange, especially the London Stock Exchange.

jobber's turn The difference between the prices at which a jobber is willing to buy and sell securities.

joint account 1. In banking, an account held in the name of two or more people, any or all of whom may have full powers to operate the account, either with the others or on their own. 2. In business, a venture jointly undertaken by two or more individuals or firms, who share all costs, profits and losses.

joint and several Legal term meaning that the parties

to an agreement are to be held responsible both jointly, i.e. as a group, and also individually, for the fulfilment of the whole of the agreement.

joint consultation Discussion between employers and representatives of employees of matters of joint concern such as the future policy of the business. Matters which are normally the subject of *collective bargaining* are usually meant to be excluded from this process although in practice this is often not possible.

joint cost Cost incurred in the production of *joint products*, i.e. products with some common stages of production, during these stages of production.

joint stock banks A term formerly used to distinguish the 'High Street' retail banks which were public companies from the London merchant banks which were often partnerships. As most banks are now limited companies and many of them are financial conglomerates covering a wide range of activities in several retail and wholesale finance markets, the term is passing out of use.

joint stock company A corporation with its capital divided into many small units of shares or stock which may be held by a number of investors. In the UK the term is virtually synonymous with 'limited company' but in the USA the liability of shareholders in 'joint stock companies' is unlimited.

joint tenants Two or more owners who hold real or personal property in plurality, together making up the owner and each having rights in the whole of the property.

joint works committee In a factory, a committee of management and worker representatives who meet to discuss matters of common concern.

journal Originally a daily record of business transactions, the term is now used more generally for a record of financial transactions such as transfers between accounts and for corrections of accounting mistakes.

judgment creditor A person who has brought an action for debt or damage against another in a court of law and who has obtained judgment for the whole or part of the amount claimed.

judgment debtor One who has been ordered by a court of law to pay a sum of money to another, the creditor.

justification The process of arranging a line of text, often by adjusting the spaces between letters or words, so that there is a straight line of text along the left, right or both margins.

K

K In computing, a unit of 1024 bytes. In colloquial use to mean 'one thousand', especially one thousand dollars or pounds. It sometimes appears in the same sense in job advertisements.

keep house A debtor is said to 'keep house' if he or she refuses to see creditors even though they call at reasonable hours.

kerb market An unofficial market in stocks and shares, especially one trading outside official hours.

keyboard A collection of switches, keys, buttons or marked areas on a board used to communicate with a typing, printing or processing device or system. Each press on a key is a *keystroke*.

kite 1. An *accommodation bill*. 2. A cheque drawn on a bank account with insufficient funds to meet it. 3. Now, more especially, a cheque.

kiteflying Dealing in fictitious or accommodation bills in order to raise money to keep up one's credit.

kitemark A kite-shaped mark that may be placed on items to signify that they have been approved by the British Standards Institution.

knock-for-knock In motor insurance, an agreement between insurers that each will pay the accidental vehicle damage claims of its own policyholders instead of pursuing a mass of expensive legal enquiries to establish individual liabilities.

L

labour (labor) Physical or mental work contributing to economic production.

labour cost Cost to the firm of employing labour, taking into account such items as taxes, national insurance contributions and other compulsory payments to the State.

labour, direct Labour expended in altering the composition, condition, conformation or construction of the product.

labour, indirect Labour expended which does not alter the composition, condition, conformation or construction of the product.

labour intensive Production operations requiring a high proportion of labour to capital (machines).

laches A legal term for neglect in regard to delay, usually of such a nature as to be prejudicial to the rights of the person who has been negligent.

lacuna Gap or something missing in a document.

laden weight The weight of a vehicle and its load.

LAFTA Latin American Free Trade Association.

lame duck An expression used on a stock exchange to point out a defaulter who, being unable to meet his obligations, is 'hammered' and expelled from the house (the exchange).

laminated Made up from a series of layers of metal, wood, plastic or other material.

land One of the traditional factors of production in economics. It is used in two senses: 1. the space required for a production process to take place; 2. the basic or raw materials from land, sea or air before being worked on or processed for production.

Land Register A national register of titles to land.

land waiter A Customs officer who tastes, weighs, measures and examines goods liable to duty and takes an account of them for the purposes of taxation, on their being landed from a ship; or in the case of exported goods, who watches over and certifies that the goods are shipped in accordance with the prescribed form. Also a *landing officer* and a *searcher*.

landing order A Customs document addressed to the chief officer of a ship, after duty liabilities have been cleared on the goods imported, authorizing the officer to unload goods. The goods are inspected by the landing officer as they leave the ship and the officer signs the landing order to indicate that entry is correct.

landlord Person who lets land or property to a tenant.

larceny The legal term for theft.

laser disk A video disk from which information is read by means of a laser light beam. The data is recorded as a series of pitted tracks. As the light hits the tracks it is reflected to a reading head which converts the variations in the reflected light into electrical signals. Optical systems such as this are not sensitive to surface contamination and there is no mechanical contact between head and disk surface to cause wear.

laser scanning The use of laser to read bar codes on stock, etc., and feed the information to a computer for management use.

launder To convert money obtained illegally into a form whereby it can be used legally.

law agent A Scots term for a person entitled to practise in the law courts.

law merchant The usages and customs which regulate matters relating to commerce. Also *lex mercatorum*

lay days A shipping term for the number of days allowed for loading and unloading ships as stipulated in the charter party.

lay off 1. To discharge workers temporarily. 2. To spread a heavy risk over a number of insurance companies and/or Lloyd's underwriters so that no single insurer will have to face the possibility of suffering a crippling burden.

lay person A practitioner who is non-professional, non-expert, lacking informal qualifications, an outsider.

LDC Less developed country. One with a low national income per head of population.

lead An insurance term for the proportion of a risk that the principal underwriter is prepared to accept and the terms of his acceptance.

lead time The time interval between planning and first production of a new product.

leading indicator Economic data believed to predict approaching economic trends or events.

leakage An allowance made for waste or loss in liquids.

lease A legal agreement relating to the use or possession of land, property or equipment for a period of time. Leasing has become an accepted method of acquiring capital equipment. Under a *cross-border lease* an equipment manufacturer may sell to a home leasing company which then leases the goods to a foreign firm. Under a *local lease* the manufacturer would sell to a foreign leasing company for lease to a firm in the foreign country.

lease-back (also *sale and lease-back*) The practice whereby a firm sells freehold land or property to a financial institution but keeps possession under the terms of a long lease. The object is to release capital for use in the business.

leasehold Real estate held under the terms of a lease.

LEC Local export control. An arrangement with Customs authorities whereby regular exporters can gain clearance for export, usually of containers, from their own premises.

ledger The main book or set of books used to record

trading transactions and in which debtor-creditor accounts are summarized.

legacy Property, etc., left to a person or organization under the terms of a will.

legal aid In the UK, financial assistance authorized by statute to enable people with very low incomes to obtain qualified representation in legal disputes.

legal day In law the day ends at midnight.

legal tender Forms of money which must be accepted when offered in settlement of a debt. In the UK Bank of England notes and the £1 coin are legal tender without limit as are gold coins and maundy money. Other coins are limited legal tender with the limits of acceptance established by statute.

legatee The person who receives a legacy.

legation The official residence of a nation's diplomatic representatives.

lender of last resort A country's central bank.

lessee The person to whom a lease is granted.

lessor The person who grants a lease.

letter of allotment A letter sent to the applicant for shares in public companies stating the number of shares that have been allotted in response to the application.

letter of attorney A legal document authorizing one person to act on behalf of another in accordance with the terms of the letter.

letter of credit A letter from bankers or mercantile houses, addressed to their agent or correspondent, at home or abroad, requesting money to be advanced to the bearer against the writer's account, subject to the terms of the letter.

letter of hypothecation The letter of authority given to a bank under a documentary credit whereby the bank is authorized to dispose of the goods if the consignee fails to meet commitments. Without such a letter the bank has no right to goods subject to a bill of exchange.

letter of indemnity A letter sent by one person or organization to another or others undertaking to accept the liability for any claim or loss on the happening of some specified event or events.

letter of indication A form of identification to be carried by the payee when a circular note or letter of credit is issued.

letter of introduction A letter addressed by banks, mercantile houses and others to their agents, correspondents or friends, at home or abroad, introducing the bearer of the letter to them and stating that any assistance or information given to the bearer will be taken as a personal favour to the writer.

letter of regret A letter sent to the applicant for shares in public companies, in cases where the number of shares applied for is greater than the number issued and stating that no allotment has been made in respect of the application.

letter of renunciation A form printed with an allotment letter and which can be used to transfer rights to shares to another.

letterbox company A company registered in a particular country solely for the purpose of avoiding or reducing liability to taxes.

letterpress The process of printing from a raised surface such as type, blocks or plates.

letters of administration The authority granted to an approved person to administer the estate of a dead person who has not left a will.

letter of credit Letter authorizing a bank to make a payment or payments or to release an accepted bill of exchange, subject to the satisfactory fulfilment of specified conditions. The term is most frequently found in relation to the *documentary credit* system of making payments in international trade. Letters of credit may be 'revocable', i.e. may be cancelled by the payer alone, or 'irrevocable', i.e. may be cancelled or changed only by agreement of both parties. Banks will normally deal only with irrevocable letters of credit.

letters patent A privilege granted by the State giving a person the sole legal right to make use of an invention or discovery for a period of years established by patents legislation. They are 'letters patent' because they are open and addressed to the world in general.

level of living (USA) Equivalent of standard of living (UK). This refers chiefly but not exclusively to the level of goods and services available to the average person in a community.

leverage (USA) Equivalent to UK *gearing*, i.e. the ratio of debt to *common stock* (ordinary shares) in the capital structure of a company.

lex mercatorum also (lex mercatoria or the *law of merchants*) In a general sense this relates to the usages and customs which regulate matters concerning commerce. See also *law merchant*.

liabilities The legal obligations or debts owed by a person or organization or likely to arise from their activities.

LIC Local import control. An arrangement with Customs authorities whereby regular importers may obtain entry of their goods, usually by container, locally and have them cleared at their own premises.

licence (license, especially USA) Formal authorization by an appropriate authority, especially the government or its agents, to do specified things, or own specified articles, as drive a car, fish, sell alcohol or own a dog.

licensed dealer A dealer in securities licensed by the Department of Trade but not a member of the Stock Exchange.

licensed deposit taker A financial institution operating in the United Kingdom licensed by the Bank of England to accept deposits but not permitted to call itself a bank nor to undertake wider banking functions.

lien A legal right to detain goods belonging to another until the charges upon them have been paid, or until some pecuniary claim against the owners has been satisfied.

lien maritime The right, independent of possession, to a ship wherever it may be. This right may arise out of an adventure at sea and, if necessary, may be enforced by arrest and sale.

life annuity An annuity payable to a person for the duration of his or her life.

life assurance That class of insurance business which is concerned with the financial risks associated with human life and death.

life interest An interest in property lasting during a person's lifetime.

LIFFE London International Financial Futures Exchange. A London market for speculation and hedging transactions in certain currencies and financial securities.

LIFO last in first out. A system of stock valuation which assumes that stock is consumed in reverse order to its purchase.

light dues Tolls levied on a ship towards the maintenance of lights, beacons, buoys and other navigational aids to shipping.

light pen In computing, a penlike input device that is used with a cathode ray tube display. It can be used to point to areas on the screen and indicate a selection from a displayed list or it can be used to draw and manipulate shapes. The light pen has a photo-sensor at its tip which is able to detect the peak illumination which occurs when the cathode rate tube scanning spot passes its point of focus. A switch, usually on the pen, is used to indicate the intended start and finish of any drawing action.

limit A fixed price given by principal to agent for the purchase or sale of some kind of property.

limitation of actions The fixed period defined by statute during which legal actions may be commenced.

limited liability The privilege whereby shareholders of a limited company are liable only for the subscribed amount of their shares.

limited partnership A partnership conforming to rules established by statute and where all but one of the partners, subject to certain conditions, may enjoy the privilege of limited liability for the debts and obligations of the firm.

line An insurance term, especially at Lloyd's, indicating the proportion of a risk that an underwriter is prepared to accept.

line authority or management A management term denoting the direct line of responsibility from the head of an organization through subordinates to the managers actually providing the organization's product or service.

line of credit An international trade term for a loan made by a bank in one country to a bank or

liquid assets Assets are said to be liquid when they can be swiftly and surely converted to cash or spendable bank credit.

liquid capital Sometimes used for liquid physical assets but more generally for short term borrowings that may have to be repaid at short notice.

liquidation The settlement or closing up of all business transactions, or the winding-up of a company or business.

liquidator One who is charged with the responsibility for liquidating a company or business.

liquidity The quality of being liquid.

liquidity ratio The term commonly applied to the ratio of defined liquid assets of a bank to certain customer deposits.

listed company A company whose shares are listed in the stock exchange's official list and which are traded on the main exchange.

lithography Originally a process of reproduction whereby marks were made on stone from which inked impressions could be taken. Later the process involved metal plates instead of stone. In 'direct litho' the impression is conveyed directly from the plate to paper. In 'offset litho' the image is first printed on some other substance from which it is transferred to the paper copy.

liveryman A freeman of the City of London, who is entitled to wear the livery and enjoy the privileges of his company.

Lloyd's An international insurance market in London. Individual underwriters are grouped in syndicates and accept unlimited liability for risks accepted in their names.

LME London Metal Exchange. A London market for trading in metals and metal futures.

load line The line marked on a ship's hull indicating the extent to which the ship is permitted to sink when loaded. Also known as the *Plimsoll line*.

load lists A Customs term for the detailed lists of consignments of goods for export. They normally include details of vessel or flight number, expected date of sailing or flight, destination, description of goods, number of packages and marks and numbers on packages.

loader A Customs term which usually denotes the carrier, normally the shipping line or airline, responsible for the international carriage of exported goods. It includes anyone who carries out the function of receiving goods and documents from exporters and agents, presenting them to Customs and actually placing them on the ship or aircraft. The loader is responsible for providing Customs with accurate and complete information and for following correct procedures, including presentation of *load lists*.

loan capital The total amount of money borrowed by a firm. See also *debt capital*.

loan stock That part of the loan capital which is in the form of transferable securities on which a fixed rate of interest is payable. Loan stock may be 'secured' in which case the stock holders have a charge on specific assets or a floating charge on the physical assets of the firm, or they may be 'unsecured' in which case the stock holders have no special rights to the value of the assets.

local area network A communication network linking a number of workstations in the same local area which may be: the same building, a radius of about 1 kilometre, or in the area of a single manufacturing plant. The system enables individual computers or workstations to send messages and files to each other and to share devices such as printers, disk storage and access to other computers.

lock out The practice of employers in refusing entry to the workplace to workers with whom they are in dispute.

loco An old price term whose modern equivalent is *ex-works*, i.e. the buyer pays all transport costs.

locum tenens A deputy or substitute, or one who acts for and represents another during that person's absence.

log-book The official record kept by the master of a ship. Sometimes used to refer to the registration document of a motor vehicle.

logging on The process by which the user of a

computer to which access is restricted or controlled identifies him- or herself to a system.

logo An abbreviation of logogram, a single distinctive sign or character to represent the trade name or mark of an organization.

Lombard Street A term used to refer to the London money market because so many banks are situated there.

long (USA) The practice of buying goods or financial securities in anticipation of a price rise. Equivalent to the stock market term *bull*.

long dated stock Government securities with over fifteen years to run to the date of maturity.

loss adjuster A professional person who negotiates the settlement of insurance claims. See *average adjuster*.

loss leader Stock offered for sale at a very low price to tempt customers in anticipation that they will buy additional goods.

lot An item, set or group of items offered for separate sale at an auction.

low geared A term used to describe the capital structure of a company with a low proportion of debt to its ordinary share capital.

low level language A variety of programming language in which the control and data structures directly reflect the specifications of the computer system.

Ltd (Limited) Companies which in the UK have the word 'limited' or a recognized abbreviation, or the equivalent in Welsh, are private limited companies as defined by the Companies Acts.

luck money Small rebate made following a cash bargain to maintain goodwill.

lumber (USA) timber, (UK) bulky and worthless material, clutter.

lump Originally a payment made for work by a lump sum rather than by regular weekly or monthly wages as a device to avoid tax and other statutory payments, this term is applied more generally, but especially in the building trade, for work arranged on a sub-contract rather than employer-employee basis, still with the main aim of avoiding or reducing employment taxes.

luncheon voucher A note issued to an employee authorizing approved traders to charge the employer with the cost of food bought by the employee up to a stated limit. These vouchers may gain a local circulation as token money.

M

MAC Minister's approval certificate. A certificate required before first licensing for most goods vehicles made outside the European Communities and which have an unladen weight greater than one thousand five hundred and twenty-five kilograms.

machine language A computer program which is embedded in the computer itself.

made bill A bill which has the name of a third party on it in the form of one or more endorsers.

mail order A retailing system whereby goods or services are ordered by post in response to advertising by newspaper, catalogue or other means.

mail shot An advertisement communicated to a large group of possible buyers by post.

mail transfer An international money transfer whereby money is transferred from a bank account in one country to another bank account in another country and the necessary instructions between the banks are communicated by air mail.

mainframe computer A large computer with considerable capacity and capable of complex operations.

make a turn Achieve a profit by buying something,

especially stocks and shares, and selling at a higher price.

making-up day The first day of the period allowed for settlement in the stock exchange.

making-up price The price at which shares are closed for current settlement in the stock exchange and the basis for the opening price for the next account.

management accounting The systematic application of the techniques and principles of accounting to assist the management of a business enterprise in the formulation of policies and in the planning and control of the business.

management by objectives A management system based on the assessment of performance measured against mutually agreed objectives

management consultant A person who offers skilled advice on business management problems.

management information system An information system whose main purpose is to supply information to managers. The tendency in modern systems is to allow managers to gain access to the system themselves to seek and manipulate whatever information they require.

management ratio One of the accounting ratios which indicate the financial position of the firm and its operations and which can be used as a basis for management decisions. Examples include the working capital ratio, the ratio of net profit to sales revenue or the ratio of net profit to capital employed in the business.

mandate Formal authority to a person or organisation to act according to specific instructions.

manifest A detailed list of cargo carried by a ship, aircraft or road vehicle or in a container. It is signed by or on behalf of whoever is in charge of the transport vehicle or craft, e.g. a ship's manifest is signed by or on behalf of the ship's master. Ship's manifests of cargo to be exported must be submitted to Customs within fourteen days of clearance outwards of the vessel. Aircraft manifests must be submitted when applying for aircraft clearance.

manpower planning Systematic recruitment, training and personnel management designed to ensure that worker availability will match the future needs of the business organization.

margin 1. An additional amount to allow for contingencies. 2. An amount deposited with a broker to meet possible transaction losses. 3. Difference between buying and selling price. 4. The physical boundary of text as it appears on paper or on a computer or word processor's visual display.

margin dealing Speculative dealing in shares or commodities with a percentage of the price deposited as a margin.

marginal Term used in economics to denote a change in the total of one variable resulting from a small change in another.

marginal cost The change in total cost as quantity produced changes.

marginal product The change in total quantity produced resulting from a change in the quantity used of one or more production resources.

marginal revenue The change in total revenue as total quantity sold changes.

marine insurance That class of insurance business that is concerned with covering risks associated with ships or their cargoes.

maritime law That branch of commercial law that is concerned with ships and services to shipping.

marked checks (USA) Cheques marked by the banks on which they have been drawn as sure to be paid when presented. See also *certified cheques*.

market 1. Area within which buyers and sellers of identifiable goods, services or resources are able to communicate. 2. The activity of buying and selling, as in 'active market'. 3. The demand for an identifiable 'good'.

market appraisal The systematic investigation of the influences affecting the demand for a particular product or products.

market economy An economic system where the institutions of production and distribution are mostly in private ownership and control and the 'what, how and for whom' production decisions are left as much as possible to the unregulated forces of demand and supply in the market.

market overt A market in which goods are openly displayed for sale to all who may wish to buy.

market profile The main features relating to the demand for a particular product or products.

market research The systematic investigation of market conditions.

market segmentation The identification of differing sections of a product market so that differing marketing strategies can be applied.

market value The price obtainable by open sale.

marketing The business activity that links production to market requirements and which seeks to influence market attitudes in the producer's favour.

marketing mix The combination of strategies relating to price, advertising, distribution channels, etc., available for product marketing.

marking On a stock exchange, the recording of prices at which business has been done during the official hours of trading.

mark-up The addition to cost price to produce selling price. Equivalent to *margin (3)*.

Martinmas A Scottish quarter day, the 11th of November.

mass produced Produced on a large scale with an implication of 'sameness' and lack of individuality.

mate An officer on a merchant ship executing the master's orders and able to take command in his absence.

material Adjective meaning significant, of importance.

material fact A legal insurance term meaning a fact that would influence a prudent underwriter in the decision whether or not to provide cover for a risk or the premium to be charged for cover.

matrix management A system of organizational management based on project teams drawn from two or more functional departments.

maturity The date when an obligation to pay under a bill, bond, loan or other financial security is due.

MD Managing director. An executive director of the company, usually the principal executive, whose powers are normally established in the company's articles of association.

measured-day work A system which combines elements of *payment by results* with normal time based pay whereby an agreed standard is established for the work expected for a day and pay is set at a higher than normal rate.

media A term commonly used to refer to the national media of communications, including television and radio networks and the national press.

medium-dated securities Government securities whose maturity date is more than five years but less than fifteen years in the future.

memorandum of association The document which, in the UK, defines the identity, share capital and powers of a company and its status as private or public, in accordance with the detailed provisions of the Companies Acts.

memory In computing a device or medium that can retain information for subsequent retrieval. Although the term may be used in the general sense of a store it is most frequently used to refer to the internal store within the computer to which access can be gained directly by an operating instruction. 'Loading a program or file into memory' usually refers to the transfer of information from a disk to the internal storage of the computer.

menu A list displayed on a computer of processing options from which a choice can be made.

mercenary Motivated purely by thought of financial gain.

mercer A merchant dealing in textiles, especially silks and cloth of high value.

merchandizing The business techniques associated with product distribution and sale.

merchant One who trades in goods on own account for profit. The term is used chiefly in the wholesale trades and especially in foreign trade, e.g. *export-import merchant*.

merchant banking A general description of a range of banking and financial services, offered mainly to large or growing business organizations. These services usually include the acceptance of bills of exchange, assistance with meeting the financial needs of the business and generally playing an active and entrepreneurial role in financial advice and management.

merchantable quality A legal term used in British sale of goods legislation to refer to the condition of goods sold. Goods not of merchantable quality are not fit for sale.

merger A joining together of two firms.

messuage A legal term denoting a dwelling house with its outbuildings and adjacent land.

method study The systematic study of work processes with a view to improving their efficiency. Similar in meaning to *time and motion study*.

MIB Motor Insurers' Bureau. An organization set up by motor insurers in the UK to deal with personal injury claims resulting from uninsured motor accidents.

MICR Magnetic Ink Character Recognition. A process of marking cheques and other paper instruments to aid computerized sorting.

microcomputer A general term describing a computer from 'desk-top' to pocket or smaller size. It uses a *microprocessor* as its central control and arithmetic element.

microfiche A single sheet of film containing a large

number of individual records which can be viewed through a viewer or 'reader'.

microfilm The process whereby paper records are photographed and stored on film in a very much reduced form.

micrographics The use of microfilm techniques and systems for the handling of records and files.

microprocessor A semiconductor chip, or chip set, that implements the central processor of a computer.

middleman A trader who acts as an intermediary between two other business organizations.

minicomputer A computer which is larger than a micro- or desk top model but which is not large enough to be termed 'mainframe'.

minimum lending rate See *MLR*

minimum subscription The minimum amount which, in the opinion of a company's directors must be raised by an issue of shares to provide: the purchase price of property; preliminary expenses of the issue; underwriting commissions; repayment of money borrowed; working capital.

minor A young person below a certain age and having limited or no legal liability, as stipulated by the law of a country. This age varies from nation to nation.

minority interests Those individual stockholdings in a *subsidiary company* and which in total form a minority, powerless to influence the control exercised by the majority held by the *holding company*. The interests of the *minority shareholders* are protected to some extent by company law.

minutes The report of the proceedings of a meeting, intended to form part of a continuous record.

misrepresentation The deliberate or careless communication of false information.

mitigate To reduce the severity or seriousness of something.

mixed economy An economic system in which the ownership and control of the institutions of production and distribution are shared between the State and private citizens.

MLR minimum lending rate. In the UK this is the formally announced rate at which the Bank of England will re-discount first class bills and securities. The Bank reserves the power to activate MLR during periods when its regular use is suspended.

MMC Monopolies and Mergers Commission. A body charged with responsibility for investigating and reporting on monopolies and mergers in the UK when requested to do so by the government.

mode Style or fashion. Used by computer staff to denote a particular pattern of computer operation.

model A simplified representation of an aspect of the

real world used to assist investigation and understanding of the real world.

monetarism A term applied to a school of economic thought which lays stress on the preservation of 'sound' money and strict financial discipline, including controlling the money supply. In more recent times the term has also been more loosely applied to a political-economic philosophy which seeks to minimize State intervention in economic production and distribution.

monetary base The quantity of notes and coin circulating in the economy together with the quantity held in the banking sector.

monetary sector In the UK this is defined as those banks recognized as full banks by the Bank of England, deposit taking institutions also licensed as such by the Bank of England, the trustee savings banks and the banking department of the Bank of England.

money Any financial instrument that is acceptable as payment in a trading transaction. In the UK money is defined and measured according to a series of 'monetary aggregates' the most common of which are: M0, M1 (the measures of *narrow money*), M3, £M3, PSL2. (Private Sector Liquidity 2) (the measures of *broad money*). The principal measures in the USA, going from narrow to broad are: M1-A, M1-B, M2, M3. and L.

money at call Loaned money which can be recalled immediately without any period of notice. See also *call money*.

money illusion Actions and attitudes consistent with a belief that money has retained a degree of purchasing power that, in practice, it has lost.

Money Market The term usually used to describe the market in very short term money, especially in the City of London.

money shop A business which offers a range of financial advisory, management and lending services mostly to individuals and very small firms.

monitor 1. A visual display screen which accepts a video signal and provides better graphics definition than a television receiver. 2. A part or complete operating system which examines the processes being carried out by a computer system and takes action if necessary.

monopoly A market in which supply is controlled by one supplier or by a single group of suppliers acting together.

moonlighting Undertaking paid work outside one's normal full-time occupation. There is sometimes an implication of income tax evasion.

moratorium An extension of time allowed for the repayment of a debt.

mortgage The conveyance of a legal or an equitable interest in real or personal property as security for a debt.

mortgage debenture Loan stock which is secured on specific property. In the event of failure to honour the terms of the debenture its holders are entitled to the proceeds of the sale of the secured property

mortgagee One to whom a mortgage is made or given.

mortgagor One who grants a mortgage.

motion A proposal in definite terms, put before a meeting with a view to its adoption as a resolution.

moving average An average obtained by selecting a number of consecutive values in a series and averaging these in order to reduce the variations in individual values and identify a trend.

MP Months after payment

MPC Marginal propensity to consume. The proportion of a change in total income which is related to consumption.

MPM Marginal propensity to import. The proportion of a change in total income which is spent on imports.

MPS Marginal propensity to save. The proportion of a change in total income which is saved.

M/R Mate's receipt. A receipt given by a ship's mate for goods received on board ship.

MS Manuscript. Strictly this means something written by hand but the term is now loosely applied to the original of work submitted for printing whether hand written, typed or prepared by word processor.

MSC Manpower Services Commission. A British government agency with training and employment responsibilities.

multi-access system A system allowing several users to make apparently simultaneous use of a computer. Each user is connected to the main system by a terminal.

multinational company A company which has direct ownership and control over the production of goods or services in more than one country.

multiple store A retail organization with more than one branch establishment.

multiplier In economics this relates to the ratio of a total change in an aggregate such as money or national income, to an initial change in one of the elements in that aggregate such as a new bank deposit or new injection of investment or government expenditure.

mutual fund (USA) A financial institution chiefly concerned with investment.

mutual society An organization formed to transact business of a particular type, as life assurance, where the customers are the legal owners and are entitled to share in the profits of the enterprise.

N

na Not applicable; not available.

name The term given to an investing member of Lloyd's who is one of an underwriting syndicate and who takes an agreed share in the risks, profits and losses of that syndicate. Each name has to accept unlimited personal liability for losses.

name day The second day of the stock exchange settlement. Also called *ticket day*.

narrow money Totally liquid money. In the UK defined by the measures M0 and M1.

national debt Total accumulated borrowings of the government of the country.

National Economic Development Council An institution in the UK through which leaders of the government, private sector business and the trade unions meet and discuss current economic and business problems. Its work is administered through the National Economic Development Office.

National Girobank A State-owned bank in the UK which offers mainly money transfer services and which makes extensive use of Post Office facilities.

national income Sometimes used loosely to refer to the total value of a nation's economic activity during the year but more strictly the measurement of the gross national product less a deduction for the amount of the nation's capital consumed during the year. See also *net national product*.

national savings certificates British government securities for money borrowed from the public. They are issued in small denominations through the post offices and interest is accumulated on a tax-free basis and paid when the principal is repaid. Individual holdings are subject to limits.

nationalization The taking over by the State of privately owned and controlled business organizations.

nationalized industries Sectors of economic activity, operated by organizations which are owned and controlled by the State and specifically designated as nationalized industries, as opposed to other public sector agencies.

naturalization The process whereby an alien resident obtains the citizenship of his or her adopted country.

near money Assets which do not have the total liquidity and acceptability of 'true money' but which are very close to this. The term used to be applied to bank seven day deposits but has been largely supplanted by the use of 'narrow' and 'broad' definitions of money.

negligence Failure to observe a reasonable standard of care.

negotiable instrument also

negotiable paper A document or form of payment such as a cheque or a bank note which is transferable and to which the person who takes it in good faith and for value gains a good title regardless of any possible defects in the title of the transferor.

negotiating bank The bank which negotiates under the terms of a credit.

negotiation The purchase of a bill of exchange or other document of title.

neo- A prefix signifying 'a later revival of..' as in 'neoclassical economics' and 'neomonetarism'.

net or **nett** 1. The total amount remaining after all deductions have been made. 2. The actual amount with no deductions allowable.

net domestic product The *gross domestic product* less an allowance for capital depreciation during the period.

net national product The gross national product less an allowance for the consumption of the nation's capital during the year. See also *national income*.

net present value The *present value* of an investment project less its estimated cost.

net profit The earnings remaining to an organization when all payments and liabilities to make payments have been allowed for.

net worth also *net assets* The value of the excess of an organization's assets over its liabilities.

network In communications, a loosely defined term applied to any system consisting of terminals *nodes* and interconnecting media. The interconnections can take a variety of forms including: line, radio waves and satellites.

network analysis A form of management planning which identifies the sequence and timing of related operations and seeks to co-ordinate these in the most efficient way. See also *critical path analysis* and *PERT*.

new deal (USA) A term referring to various aspects of the economic revival programmes instituted by President Roosevelt after the economic crash of 1929.

new issue market That section of the capital market which is concerned with the provision of long-term finance to business and public sector organizations through issues of new or additional shares or loan stocks.

new shares Shares which can be transferred using one of the temporary evidences of ownership known as the *renounceable documents*.

new time The term applied to stock exchange transactions arranged in the last two days of an accounting period but which, by agreement, are deemed to have taken place in the next account.

NIC Newly industrialized countries. A group of rapidly industrializing former developing countries.

NIT Negative income tax. A system of payment of income by the State to individuals with low incomes to bring their incomes up to a specific minimum level.

night safe A deposit box from which access is gained by those with the necessary key, through a covered opening in a bank's wall. It enables customers to deposit cash when the bank is closed for normal business.

nil paid A new issue of shares on which no payment has so far been made. This usually relates to a *rights issue*.

NLRB National Labor Relations Board (USA). A five member Board appointed by the President and set up to implement the Wagner Act of 1935 recognizing the rights of trade unions in the USA.

node A connection point or junction within a *network* where two or more devices are linked together. They are also known as stations and exchanges.

noise In communications, electronic and other, any signal or message which is extraneous to and distracts attention from, the signal being communicated.

nominal accounts The accounts which represent and record the character and amount of profits or losses, income and expenses.

nominal amount or

nominal payment A small amount simply to signify that a payment has been made.

nominal capital The amount of the capital of a joint-stock company authorized by its memorandum of association. See also *authorized capital*

nominal price The nearest market value of goods or securities in which there is little trade.

nominal value The face or unit value stated for a security but which bears no relationship to the market value.

nominee 1. One on whose life an annuity or lease depends. 2. One named in a transaction instead of the real person concerned.

nonprice competition Business competition using advertising, promotional campaigns, special terms for distributors and other means rather than price reductions.

nonunion shop A working establishment where management neither recognizes nor negotiates with trade unions.

normative Concerned with standards, hence a concern with what 'ought to be' rather than with 'what is'. A term applied to statements and to studies in the social sciences.

not negotiable If this term is written on a cheque or other instrument of payment then anyone to whom the instrument is transferred cannot receive a better title than that possessed by the transferor. It does not prevent transfer but, in practice, many commercial and financial offices will refuse to take an endorsed cheque marked in this way in payment.

notary public A specially authorized person who attests, copies, or translates certain documents and writings, or proves their validity for the purpose of giving them effect abroad, and whose business it is to present dishonoured bills of exchange, and *protest* and note their non-acceptance or non-payment.

note of hand A document promising payment of a named sum of money at a particular date.

notify party The person or organisation to be informed when goods have arrived. This party's name and address are normally shown on transport documents used in foreign trade and they must appear on transport (shipping) documents which form part of a *documentary credit*.

noting a bill Presentation of a bill of exchange for payment by a notary public after it has been returned dishonoured with the object of formally noting (recording) non-payment preparatory to *protest*.

NPV (Net present value) The *present value* of an additional profit or stream of additional profits due in the future and resulting from an investment project, less the cost of that project.

nurse an account 1. In banking this means to retain a security received as backing for a loan commitment whose terms are not being met in the hope that the loan will eventually be repaid or the security increase in marketable value. 2. In more general business use the term is used to mean giving very special attention to a particular customer in the hope that he or she will become a source of more valuable business in the future.

NYSE Index (New York Stock Exchange Index) A market price index of a wide range of stocks traded on the New York Stock Exchange.

O

O & M Organization and methods. The systematic study of office work with a view to increasing efficiency.

obscuration The amount of proof spirit hidden, or 'obscured' by matter in solution in a spirituous liquor, i.e. the difference between the true or actual strength and that indicated by a hydrometer.

OECD Organization for Economic Co-operation and Development. A group of mostly advanced industrialized nations, sometimes referred to as the 'rich man's club' of nations.

off licence 1. A licence to sell liquor which is not to be consumed on the premises. 2. A retail establishment holding such a licence.

off-board market (USA) The American term for a market in shares outside the regular stock exchanges. The equivalent of the UK *over-the-counter market*.

offer 1. The first step in the process of concluding a trading contract in which a willingness to enter into a specific agreement is communicated to another. 2. An indication of willingness to sell shares or other financial securities at a particular price.

offer for sale A public issue and the document

containing the terms of a public issue, made by an issuing house, of shares which it has bought from the company.

official dispute or **strike** An industrial dispute which is officially recognized and supported within the rules of the trade union(s) to which the workers in dispute belong. The distinction between 'official' and 'unofficial' is sometimes more apparent than real because union rules may require lengthy procedures and disputes are settled before formally being declared 'official'.

official list The Stock Exchange Daily Official List, a list of all the companies whose shares are authorized to trade on the main market of the British Stock Exchange.

official receiver A public officer appointed in the UK by authority of the Department of Trade to wind up the affairs of a bankrupt person or an insolvent company.

OFT Office of Fair Trading. A department of the British Government concerned with matters of consumer protection, with encouragement of competition and with raising standards of business conduct in relations with individual consumers.

Oftel Office of Telecommunications. A statutory body whose function is to represent the consumer interest in the British telecommunications industry.

OGL Open general licence.

OHMS On Her Majesty's Service. Mail from the offices of the central government of the UK bearing these letters does not have to pay the normal postage charges.

oligopoly A market in which there are few sellers in relation to the quantity of business transacted.

ombudsman An independent arbitrator to whom appeals may be made when an aggrieved person is not satisfied with the results of normal dispute proceedings. There is an ombudsman for the insurance industry.

omnium The aggregate value of the different kinds of stock which form a loan; or the united various portions of any particular fund or stock.

on consignment Goods sent on consignment to an agent are sent speculatively for the agent to sell on the best terms possible.

oncost See *overheads*.

ono Or nearest offer. An indication that the seller is prepared to bargain on the asking price.

on-stream In regular operation. A term used of new factories, processes, equipment, etc., which have completed trials and are now operating as part of a regular production process.

OPEC Organization of Petroleum Exporting Countries.

open account A transaction where goods and documents are sent directly to a trusted foreign buyer who agrees to pay within a certain period, usually 180 days after the invoice date. The method of payment is agreed in advance.

open cheque An uncrossed cheque.

open credit A letter of credit containing an unconditional request to pay money to another.

open indent An order from a foreign buyer to an agent and leaving the source of supply to the agent's discretion.

open market operations A system of monetary control based on the purchase and sale of government securities by the central bank on the open market and not just through banks.

open policy A marine insurance contract which establishes the terms and conditions under which cover is granted for cargoes transported to agreed destinations. Details of all cargoes actually transported are declared to the underwriters by the insured or broker and these form the basis for the premium to be paid.

operations research The application of scientific, particularly mathematical techniques to the solution of business problems, especially those requiring a 'best possible' solution subject to certain known limitations or constraints and given goals.

opportunity cost The cost of a product or service measured in terms of the lost opportunity to produce something else with the resources which have been used in the production process. For example, if agricultural land is used to build a motorway the opportunity cost of the motorway will include the crops that would have been grown on the land.

optical character recognition The process in which a machine, using light sensing methods, scans, recognises and encodes information printed or typed in stylised characters.

optical fibres Fibres made from special glass or plastic which enable light to be transmitted along their length by means of repeated internal reflections. As two different types of glass are used, the total internal reflection involves very little energy loss. Therefore cables consisting of many fibres can be laid in the same way as normal copper ones, yet provide more flexibility and more signal carrying capability for the same dimension of cable.

option(s) In general option means choice but in commerce it generally refers to a choice which is established as a legal right so that an option to purchase or sell property has real value and can be traded. This forms the basis for speculative and hedging deals in currency, financial futures, stock and other organized exchanges where prices are subject to constant change. Thus a trader may purchase an option to buy shares at an agreed price within an agreed period and take up the option, ie actually buy the shares if the actual price movement makes this favourable. See also *call* option and *put* option.

OR See *operations research*.

Oracle The name of the British Independent Broadcasting Authority's *teletext* service which transmits data along with normal television programme transmissions.

ordinary resolution A formal decision made at a meeting by virtue of a simple majority of those present and voting in person or by proxy.

ordinary shares or stock Company shares that have no special rights or privileges in relation to a division of profit or repayment of capital.

original bill A bill of exchange which has been drawn and sold prior to its having any endorsement.

O/S An outstanding, i.e. an unpaid, debt.

ostensible authority The authority which an agent is assumed to have from the principal by the custom and practice of the market in which they are operating.

OTC Over-the-counter. See *over-the-counter market*.

outwork Work performed at home by a worker, known as an *outworker*, as part of a production process controlled and organized by a business firm.

over-capitalized A term used to describe a business organization whose revenues are not sufficient to pay an adequate return on the full amount of capital risked in the enterprise.

overdraft The amount which a bank permits a customer to spend over the total standing to the credit of that customer's account.

overheads The cost of indirect materials, labour, administration and other expenses of operating an enterprise and which cannot be attributed directly to the production and distribution of particular products.

over-insured Where the sum insured under an insurance policy is greater than the full value of the property covered and, therefore, over the maximum amount that could be paid in compensation for an insured loss.

overnight loan Advances made in the short term money markets towards the end of the day's business and repayable, but renewable, the next day.

overriding commission Commission in addition to that due to an agent actually handling a transaction, paid to another who has had a share in, or some responsibility for arranging the deal.

overriding interests Interests in land which are not disclosed in the documents of title, for example rights of way, short leases or land taxes.

overspill A taxation term which refers to a liability for tax over the limit permitted for double taxation relief, i.e. the relief allowed for those earning income or profits in several countries and intended to ensure that the same income is not taxed twice in two countries.

oversubscription An excess of applications for shares over the amount of shares available for issue which is said to be *oversubscribed*.

over-the-counter market A market in shares outside the normal stock exchanges and which is organized and controlled by a single dealer or small group of dealers. See *off-board market*.

overtrading Dealing beyond the limit of readily available financial resources with the consequent risk of inability to meet debts as they arise.

over-valuation Used to describe a currency which is above its purchasing power parity.

own brand A brand image established by a retailer as opposed to the product manufacturer.

P

PA 1. Personal assistant. 2. Per annum, by the year.

P/A Power of attorney. See *power of attorney*.

PABX Private automatic branch exchange, an internal/external telephone system used by organizations.

package deal A complete arrangement, a term often applied to foreign holidays where the tour operator supplies a package of transport, accommodation and holiday activities.

packaging 1. The wrapping of goods. 2. The use of wrapping materials and methods to aid sales appeal and the establishment of a brand identity.

paid-up capital The amount which shareholders are deemed to have paid on the shares which have been issued and which are called up.

paid-up policy An insurance term for a life or endowment assurance policy on which premiums have ceased to be paid before the originally agreed date but the policy remains in force for a reduced sum assured.

paid-up shares Shares of a joint-stock company upon which the full nominal, face-value amount has been paid.

pallet A transportable platform used for the mechanical loading, unloading and transport of goods.

paper currency Bank notes or other documents which have the status of legal tender or which are widely acceptable as means of payment in exchange within a country.

par or **par value** Either the nominal, face value of securities or the exact amount that has been paid for them. A higher price is said to be *above par*, a lower *below par*.

par value The face value of a financial security.

parent company A company which has a controlling interest in one or more subsidiary companies and which also operates on its own account.

pari passu In equal proportions.

partial loss In marine insurance, damage or loss to ship or cargo other than total loss.

participating preference share A *preference share* which, in addition to a fixed rate of dividend has a right to a further participation in profits, usually up to a further percentage limit.

particular average In marine insurance, damage or loss which falls on one or some only of the owners of goods lost or damaged and which is not shared by all those involved in the voyage.

partly-paid share A share for which shareholders have not yet been called upon to pay the full issue price.

partners Those who join together to share the risks of a business enterprise with a view to sharing in the profits and rewards and thereby form a *partnership* which may, but need not be, formally constituted.

Pascal A computer programming language.

patent The sole right, granted by *letters patent*, to use a particular discovery for a limited period of years. This temporary monopoly is granted in exchange for disclosure of the discovery which, at the end of the period, becomes public knowledge.

patrimony Property inherited from one generation to the next. Originally from father to son but later applied in the general sense of inheritance.

pawnbroker One who advances money on the security of property deposited. This property is then said to be *pawned*. The practice is subject to conditions established by statute.

PAYE Pay as you earn. This refers to the system whereby income tax is deducted by employers on behalf of the revenue authorities to whom the tax has to be accounted for. The revenue authorities issue each income tax paying employee with a code number and the employers with tax tables indicating the amount of tax to be deducted for each code number.

payment by results Wages that depend in whole or part on the amount of production achieved by the worker either individually or as one of a team.

payment in kind A reward for work made in the form of a benefit, such as the right to use a company-owned motor vehicle, rather than as an addition to a worker's money wage or salary.

payroll tax A tax or near tax, such as British National Insurance contributions which is levied on employers of labour on the basis of the number of workers employed or on the amount of wages paid or some combination of the two.

PBX Private branch exchange. An internal/external telephone system used by organizations.

PC Personal computer.

penalty clause A contract condition that specifies payments to be made in the event of non-fulfilment of the terms of the contract, especially regarding the completion of work within a definite time period.

P/E ratio (price/earnings ratio) A measure of company performance. It is the market share price divided by the last published earnings in the form of pence per share.

peppercorn rent A purely nominal rent of a trivial amount but sufficient to meet the legal requirement that a valid contract must contain a consideration from each party.

per diem By the day.

performance bond A guarantee made by a financial institution that a contractor will complete a contract in a satisfactory manner. Failure do so will mean that the institution, the guarantor, will have to pay an agreed amount of compensation to the organization awarding the contract.

period cost See fixed cost.

perpetual annuity A yearly payment which ceases only when the *principal* is repaid.

perquisites In law these refer to fees allowed by law for specific services. When shortened to 'perks' the reference is usually to privileges with a financial value gained as a result of holding a particular rank or office.

personal loan A term often used by banks to refer to a loan to an individual customer repaid in instalments over an agreed term as opposed to the traditional bank business loan repayable in full at the end of an agreed term.

personal security A document giving the holder a claim on a person for a stated sum of money as opposed to one that gives a right to claim the value of specific property in the event of a debt not being paid.

personalized Giving the appearance of addressing a person as a distinct individual. For example, a standard advertising letter, produced by word processor, can be personalized by addressing each recipient by name.

personnel management That specialized area of management that is concerned with the recruitment, training, development and general administration relating to the people employed in an organization. It is also concerned with the implementation of the law as it relates to labour employment and dismissal and ensuring that other managers are aware of and observe that law.

PERT Programme evaluation and review technique. A form of network analysis in which each stage in a programme of work is identified with its time and its relationships to other stages. If time only is being considered the objective is to find the sequence with the least idle time – the *critical path*. When cost is introduced the objective is to find the least cost solution.

petitioning creditor A creditor who has filed a petition requesting the court to make a debtor bankrupt.

petro-currency The currency of an oil-producing nation. The currency's exchange value is strongly influenced by movements in the price of oil.

picket Representatives of a group of striking workers who gather at the entrance to a workplace in an effort to dissuade others from working. See also *secondary picket*.

pictograph 1. A representation of statistical data by means of pictorial symbols. 2. A simple pictorial symbol used to convey information, e.g. a knife and fork may indicate a place where meals can be obtained.

pie chart A method of illustrating data using a circle in which differently marked segments represent different sub-sets of a set of data. The areas of the segments are proportional to the relative sizes of the sub-sets.

piecework A term referring to a method of wage payment that is based on the number of items produced by a worker or group of workers.

pilferage A term used in shipping documents and referring to any loss caused by theft during transit.

pilotage A charge made by pilots for their services in assisting the navigation of a ship.

piracy 1. Robbery on the high seas. 2. Operating an unauthorized radio transmitter from a ship positioned outside territorial waters. 3. Unauthorized copying and commercial use of printed or otherwise recorded copyright material.

pit trading A form of market trading where all the dealers wishing to trade gather in one room and deal with each other on equal terms across the room. This form of trading is the norm in some of the older commodity exchanges which, however, also have modern telecommuniction links with outside markets and dealers.

pkg Packing or package.

placing 1. A new share issue which the *issuing house* places in blocks with its connections among the financial institutions so that no general public offer need be made. 2. Arranging for an insurance underwriter to accept the whole or a share of a risk to be covered.

plain spirits Spirits in their original state without added flavour.

plaint Statement in writing of a cause of action against another termed the *defendant*.

plaintiff One who commences and carries on a lawsuit against another.

plant Fixed machinery, implements, tools, etc., used in a production process.

PLC Public limited company. See *public limited company*.

plead 1. To deliver a pleading in a law-suit. 2. To conduct a case as an advocate.

pledge Property deposited by a borrower with a lender, especially a pawnbroker, as security for a loan.

Plimsoll line See *load line*.

plotter In computing, a device for translating information into pictorial or graphical form on paper or similar medium.

plough back A term usually used to refer to the reinvestment of profits in the business.

PN Promissory note. See *promissory note*.

POD Payment on delivery.

point of order Question raised at a meeting concerning a possible irregularity of proceedings. An immediate ruling on such a point is required from the chairman.

point-of-sale advertising The use of displays and

promotions at the place where the goods or services are actually purchased.

policy The document setting out the terms and conditions of a contract of insurance.

pony A colloquial term for £25.

port 1. A harbour or town containing a harbour where ships may dock and where cargo is loaded and unloaded. 2. An opening in a ship's side. 3. A place, not necessarily by the sea, where cargo is loaded or unloaded for transit between countries. Hence *inland port*.

porterage A charge made by dock companies for hiring porters.

portfolio The list or group of securities owned by an investor.

portfolio investment This refers to overseas investment by means of the purchase of shares and stock of foreign companies so that the investor does not gain direct control of any particular production organization.

post entry An additional entry made in relation to imported goods which were understated on the original entry.

post obit bond A bond payable only after the death of the person named in the bond.

post restante The marking on a letter to be retained at a post office until collected.

postal order An instrument of payment that can be bought and cashed at post offices.

poundage A charge or allowance, dependent on value, e.g. the charge made for the issue by the post office of a postal order.

power of attorney (P/A) A legal document giving one person the power to sign and act on behalf of another.

pp Per procurationem, on behalf of another with that person's authority, commonly used when a letter of other document is signed on behalf of another.

PR Public relations.

pratique Certificate of health issued to a ship's master by the port medical officer of health and without which a ship will not be cleared by Customs for embarkation of passengers or cargo.

precept The written warrant of a magistrate.

precis An abstract or summary of a letter or document.

predetermined cost A cost calculated before production commences.

pre-entry A declaration to the Customs authorities giving details of a consignment of goods for export.

preference stock or shares Shares which have some degree of preference over others in the payment of dividend out of profits.

preferential creditor One who has prior legal rights to have debts settled before any payment is made to others.

premium 1. An additional amount. Thus a premium wage is one above the normal wage for that type of work. A currency standing at a premium in forward trading is one that is expected to rise in value so that any agreement to sell at a future date is subject to payment of more than the rate ruling at the present time. 2. The payment made in order to obtain cover under a policy of insurance.

premium savings bonds Bonds issued by the British government and where normal interest is not payable but all bondholders take part in a draw at regular intervals. Those selected by the Electronic Random Number Indicator Equipment (ERNIE) receive prizes of varying amounts. The prizes are paid from a fund intended to represent the total interest that would have been payable under normal bond issues.

present value The discounted value of a future payment or stream of future payments payable in the future. If the present value is allowed to accumulate at rates of compound interest equivalent to the chosen rates of discount the result would be equal to the future payments.

Prestel The British *videotex* system.

price war Fierce competition involving aggressive price reductions, usually with the object of driving one or more of the competitors out of the market.

prices current A list of prices issued by traders to customers showing goods available and their present prices.

primary production Those sectors of the economy which are part of crop or animal cultivation, fishing, or any of the extractive industries such as mining and oil extraction. The products of primary production are *primary products*.

prime cost A British term equivalent to US *flat cost*. Those direct costs of production and distribution which can be attributed directly to the production or distribution of a specific product. Contrast *indirect cost*.

prime entry An entry of goods made from the particulars given on a bill of lading, invoice or other document. This may later be modified by a *post entry*.

principal 1. The head of an organization. 2. Money on which interest is paid. 3. One who authorizes an *agent*.

print-out Printed matter in readable form produced by a computer.

private company In the UK a private company is defined in the Companies Act 1985 as '...a company that is not a public company'. Private companies may be unlimited or limited by share or by guarantee. The shares of a private company cannot be offered for sale to the public. See also *limited liability, unlimited company*.

private good A product or service which provides benefits to particular persons or organizations rather than to the community as a whole.

private sector Those activities which are carried out by organizations owned and controlled by individuals or groups in the pursuit of their own private objectives.

privatization The transfer of public sector activities to the private sector.

privileges (USA) Equivalent to the British term *options*.

PRO Public relations officer. The manager charged with the general duty of ensuring that the public has a favourable attitude towards the organization.

pro forma invoice An invoice obtained for goods that a person is considering purchasing but who wishes to have full details of cost and terms of sale before reaching a final decision.

pro forma account 1. A request for payment for goods or services in advance of delivery sent to a customer when the supplier does not wish to grant that customer credit terms. 2. A fictitious account drawn up as an example or guide.

pro rata In proportion. For example, an insurance premium for three months' cover, calculated on a pro rata basis, would be one quarter of the annual premium.

probate 1. Proof of a will before the proper court. 2.

The official copy of a will with the certificate of its having been proved.

processor A computer or the central processing component of a computer.

procurator fiscal In Scotland the public prosecutor for a district.

procurement officer One who buys materials on behalf of an organization.

product differentiation The attempt to convince the public that a product has unique qualities and to distinguish it from its competitors through techniques such as distinctive packaging and creation of a brand image.

production control A form of management control in manufacturing that seeks to ensure that production processes are not hindered by such avoidable causes as shortages of materials or lack of suitable equipment.

profit and loss account One of the final accounts of a business, it is a summary record of the income and expenses of a business during a trading period. If income exceeds expenses there is a profit; if expenses are greater than income there is a loss. Equivalent to US *income statement*.

profit and loss appropriation account An account showing the disposal of the balance of the profit and loss account. Equivalent to US *retained income statement*.

program A set of statements to a computer, setting

out a series of instructions which are necessary for the computer to perform some task or calculation.

programming language An artificial language constructed in such a way that people and programmable machines can communicate with each other in a precise manner.

progress control A management control system that seeks to ensure that planned completion and delivery dates are met.

progress payment A payment made under a building or construction contract after an agreed stage in the work has been completed.

progressive tax A tax which is likely to take a larger proportion of a high than of a low income. If used to provide benefits for low income groups it may be expected to redistribute income in the direction of greater equality.

promissory note (PN) A written promise by one person, the maker, to pay to another, the payee, a definite sum of money either on demand or on a stated date. This is a formal undertaking to make a payment which can be transferred to another by *endorsement*. They are not in common use in modern trade.

promoter One who, either individually or with others, does the preliminary work, and shares the financial costs and risks of, starting an organization, such as a company, or bringing about an event, such as a boxing match.

promotion money Money paid to the promoters of a company out of the capital subscribed as compensation for their efforts. Details of any such payments must be disclosed in the *prospectus*.

prompt date or day A commodity exchange term which refers to the date on which payment is due and the buyer becomes fully responsible for goods bought at auction or by contract.

proposal form The application form for insurance cover which insurers require for certain forms of insurance cover, especially motor insurance.

A person applying for insurance is often referred to as the *proposer*.

prospectus 1. An outline of the constitution and projected plans or operations of a new company about to be formed. The prospectus must contain certain details specified by law. 2. A detailed summary of any goods or services, such as insurance, offered for sale and intended to attract customers and give them the essential information they are likely to want before coming to a decision to buy.

protection When applied to trade this refers to government attempts to limit the extent of foreign import competition which home producers have to face in domestic markets.

protest The formal attestation by a notary public of an unpaid or unaccepted foreign bill. Protest is only required when the drawer and payee are resident in different countries, but in these cases it is a necessary step before proceedings can be commenced to recover any loss.

provisional allotment letter The *allotment letter* sent to shareholders under a *rights issue* notifying them of the number of shares which they have a right to buy at the issue price.

provisions Amounts written off or retained for providing for depreciation, renewals or diminution in value of assets or retained to provide for any known liability whose amount cannot be accurately determined.

proximate cause The immediate direct cause of an event.

proxy One who acts for another, especially one authorized to attend and vote at a meeting on another's behalf.

PSD Pre-shipment document.

PSBR Public sector borrowing requirement. The amount a government needs to borrow to make up the difference between its expenditure and revenue.

PSV Public service vehicle. A vehicle permitted, usually by licence, to carry members of the public as fare-paying passengers, especially on scheduled routes.

public company or public limited company In the UK this is a company registered as such, whose distinguishing feature is that it can offer shares for sale to the general public.

public corporation The business structure whose directors are appointed by government ministers and which was devised to run nationalized industries in the UK.

public good A product or service which is of benefit to the community as a whole rather than to any individual, group or organization.

public share issue New shares offered for general sale to the public, normally through an *issuing house*.

public trustee A state official who is able to act as trustee, executor, etc., on request from members of the public.

public utilities Organizations providing basic services to the community, e.g. railways, telecommunication.

pump-priming Government spending that produces a budget deficit.

purchasing power parity A situation where the exchange rates between certain currencies are such that a given sum of money will purchase the same quantity of goods and services in each country. In this situation the *real* and the *nominal* exchange rates are the same.

put The option to sell stock or shares at an agreed price on a future date.

put and call A combined put and call arrangement. See also *straddle*.

Q

QC Quality control, a management system designed to maintain a consistent standard of product quality.

qualified acceptance An acceptance subject to conditions or qualifications. In relation to bills of exchange the acceptance may be: 1 conditional, payment depending on fulfilment of a stated condition; 2 partial, for part only of the amount named in the bill; 3 local, making the bill payable at a particular place and time only.

quango Quasi Autonomous National Government Organization. A semi-independent body set up and financed by government to fulfil functions determined by government, e.g. Monopolies and Mergers Commission, CNAA Council for National Academic Awards.

quarter days The last days of each of the quarters of the year on which payment of rent or interest traditionally became due. The English quarter days are: 1. Lady Day, March 25; 2. Midsummer Day, June 25; 3. Michaelmas, September 29; 4. Christmas, December 25. The Scottish quarter days are: 1. Candlemas, February 2; 2. Whitsun, May 15; 3. Lammas, August 1; 4. Martinmas, November 11.

quick ratio See *acid test ratio*.

quid pro quo One thing for another, a mutual favour, repayment of an obligation.

quit rent A rent on manors by which the tenants are freed from all other services.

quittance A discharge from a debt or other obligation.

quorum The minimum number of qualified persons entitled, by the rules governing the organization or group, to hold a meeting and transact business.

quota A stated quantity or proportion. When applied to foreign trade it refers to a limit, usually to imports, which a country may establish in respect of specified goods or countries.

quotation The price and terms for which a firm is prepared to supply goods or services. Unlike an estimate a quotation implies a degree of certainty and commitment and can form the basis for a legally enforceable contract.

quoted company A stock exchange term for a *listed company*, i.e. one included in the stock exchange official list and whose shares and/or debentures are traded on the main stock exchange.

R

R & D Research and development.

racking A Customs term meaning: 1. Drawing off wines or spirits from the lees or sediments; 2. Transferring wines or spirits from an unsound cask to a sound one; 3. Transferring the contents of one large cask into several smaller ones; 4. Combining the contents of several small casks into one large one.

railway consignment note A contract of carriage of goods by rail to a foreign destination. It is not a document of title and is not negotiable.

rally A recovery in prices, especially of commodity, share or stock prices.

RAM Random access memory. A computing term for a computer's memory system in which access can be gained to any desired information at will.

random sampling A scientific method of selecting a representative group from a total population that gives each member of that population an equal opportunity of selection.

rate of exchange The rate at which one currency exchanges for another in the world currency markets.

rate of return A term commonly applied to capital investment. It relates to the annual percentage *yield* on the amount invested.

rates In the UK these are local taxes levied on the owners or occupiers of land and property.

rateable value The value on which local rates are assessed. The theoretical basis is the annual rent that the property would earn on an open market but as there are no open markets for leasing many types of property, particularly private houses the rateable value has become a notional and often illogical figure.

ratification 1. Formal consent or approval often by a main body for actions or agreements made on its behalf by representatives, e.g. ratification of a negotiated wage settlement by the branches of a trade union. 2. Approval given by a principal to a contract made by an agent outside his agency powers.

rationalization The reorganization of a business and management structure in an attempt to achieve maximum efficiency.

raw materials Materials basic to the production process, including metals, minerals, or crops in their raw or natural state, before entering the production chain.

R/D (refer to drawer) The mark put on a returned cheque by a banker indicating that the drawer is unable to meet the payment.

re Concerning, in relation to, about.

real Taking into account changes in the purchasing power of money, as 'real interest', 'real price', 'real return on capital' and 'real wages'.

real accounts Accounts relating to the various business assets such as cash, plant, stock.

real cost See *cost real*.

real estate Immovable property such as land and buildings.

real time system Any system which is able to receive continuously changing data from outside sources and which is able to process the data sufficiently rapidly to be capable of influencing the sources of data. Examples include air traffic control and airline booking systems.

realization account An account opened when a business is wound up or sold as a going concern or where a partnership is being dissolved or a new partner admitted.

realty Interests in land other than leaseholds.

realtor (USA) A dealer in real estate.

rebate A discount or allowance.

received for shipment B/L A bill of lading that confirms receipt of goods for shipment by the shipping company. Its use has grown with the expansion of container traffic and the receipt by shippers of part-container loads which are dispatched to a container depot for packing with other goods to make a full container going to the same destination. The received for shipment B/L is then converted to a shipped bill by endorsement of the carrier when the goods have been loaded on board ship.

receivables The payments owing to the business.

receiver A person appointed by the court to protect the property of an estate in certain circumstances such as the insolvency or lunacy of the owner.

receiving note In the shipment of goods, a note, forming part of the shipping notes, addressed to the shipper to the chief officer of a ship, asking for the goods specified in the note to be received on board.

receiving order An order made by the Bankruptcy Court appointing an Official Receiver to take charge of and manage an insolvent person's estate for the protection of all the creditors.

reconciliation statement A statement of account whereby the balances of two accounts which show an apparent discrepancy are brought into agreement, e.g. the *bank reconciliation statement* which reconciles the cash book with the bank statement.

recorded delivery A post office service which records the transit and provides limited insurance cover for certain forms of mail.

recourse A banking term denoting the right to claim back a payment previously made.

red clause In a pre-shipment credit, the red clause authorizes the seller to obtain an advance before shipment of the goods. The advance is intended to cover the cost of shipment.

redeemable shares Shares whose terms of issue provide that the company may repurchase them under agreed conditions or at a stated time.

redemption The repayment of the amount of a financial obligation such as a debenture, mortgage, bond or share.

redemption date The date on which a security is due to be redeemed. If only the year is specified then the date is that when the last interest payment is due.

redemption yield The return that a security holder can expect based on the purchase price or present market value of the security, the annual interest and the difference between the price or market value and the amount due to be repaid at maturity.

re-draft 1. A second draft or copy. 2. A new bill of exchange which the holder of a protested bill draws on the drawer or endorsers for the amount with costs and charges.

reducing balance depreciation A system of calculating *depreciation* in which the value of a fixed asset is written down to a percentage of the previous year's value.

redundancy The dismissal of a worker on the grounds that the employer cannot provide sufficient work to justify such worker's continued employment.

redundancy fund The fund which, in the UK, is built up mainly from employers' contributions and which is used to assist employers in making statutory payments to workers made redundant.

re-exchange A charge made on the drawer of a dishonoured foreign bill of exchange by the holder on re-drawing a fresh bill.

referee 1. A person nominated by another, such as an applicant for a job, as being willing and competent to comment, i.e. give a *reference* on the other's suitability, character, creditworthiness etc. 2. One to whom some matter in dispute is referred for decision.

reflation A deliberate attempt by government to expand the level of economic activity of a country.

register A special type of store location in a computer, used for a specific purpose such as a store or an instruction register.

register of charges 1. A register, i.e., a systematic list, kept by a limited company containing particulars of loans made by the company. 2. A register of charges against land maintained at the Land Registry. 3. Register of charges against limited companies kept at the Companies Registry.

register of members The systematic list of the members of an organization. In the case of a limited liability company such a register must be kept by law and must contain details as prescribed by statute. It must be kept at the company's registered office and be available for inspection as prescribed by statute.

registered bonds Bonds which, as a protection against loss or theft, are registered in the holder's name in the books of the company or state issuing them.

registered capital See *nominal capital*.

registered land certificate A certified copy of certain particulars of an area of land extracted from the Land Register and giving evidence of title (legal claim to ownership) to that land.

registered letter Letter registered and insured by the post office and given special care in transit.

registered office The office notified to the Companies Registrar as being the registered office of the company and containing the register of members and being a place where correspondence addressed to the company may be delivered.

registered stock Stock registered in the holder's name, either by a bank or at the issuing company's office.

registered trade mark A *trade mark* which has been registered with the appropriate authorities in the user's country.

regression analysis A technique for analyzing data which seeks to identify the extent to which changes in one variable can be attributed to changes in another or others. It is used, for example, in attempts to discover the influences on the demand for a product.

re-insurance Insurance by an insurance company

with another insurer of the whole or part of a risk which has been accepted for cover by the company. This is an extension of the insurance principle of pooling or spreading of risks over a large number of people so that no one person or organization is crippled by a single loss.

release A document setting a person free from an agreement.

remainder 1. In law a residual or additional interest remaining over from an estate when this has come to an end and created by the same conveyance as that granting the estate. 2. In the book trade to sell off, at a much reduced price, unsold copies of an edition.

remainder man The person who takes the residue of an estate when the life tenant dies.

remittance Payment of a sum of money to another. The payment can take any form, including an endorsed bill of exchange.

rendu The French equivalent of 'delivered' in the internationally accepted price terms *rendu frontière* (delivered at frontier) and *rendu droits acquittés* (delivered duty paid).

renounceable certificate This is a document certifying that the holder has been allotted a stated number of new shares under the terms of a *capitalization issue* of shares, i.e. an issue made from accumulated profits and for which no payment is required. This is one of the *renounceable documents*.

renounceable documents A stock exchange term referring to the documents which constitute temporary evidence of ownership of newly issued shares. These take one of the following forms. 1. An *allotment* letter, for an ordinary sale of new shares. 2. A *provisional allotment letter* for a *rights issue*. 3. A *renounceable certificate* for a *capitalization issue*. The holder may use any of these to renounce his rights in favour or another during a specified time period.

rent Payment for the use of land, building or tenements.

rental Total rent payable during a specified period.

renter One who holds property by virtue of paying rent for it.

rentier One who derives income from ownership of property or property rights, i.e. from rents, interest, dividends, etc.

reporting a vessel 1. Giving information concerning ships sighted at sea. 2. Delivery of the *ship's report* to the Customs authorities on arrival at a port.

reputed ownership The apparent ownership of goods which have been left with one person with the owner's consent in such circumstances that they appear to belong to that person. They may be judged to belong to the holder in bankruptcy proceedings.

required reserve ratios Banking ratios involving certain assets to certain liabilities which may be

resale price maintenance The practice (now mostly illegal in the UK) of producers in forcing distributors to keep to fixed prices when re-selling goods.

rescission The legal cancellation of a contract.

reserve An appropriation of profit other than to provide for depreciation, renewals, diminution in asset value, or a retention to provide for any known liability. A reserve is established to provide for unknown contingencies.

reserve liability That portion of the uncalled capital of a limited liability company which it has resolved shall be called up only in the event of a winding-up.

reserve price Often referred to as a reserve, this is the lowest price at which a person is willing to sell goods or property, especially by public auction. The reserve is notified in advance to the auctioneer so that no effective sale can take place at a lower price without specific agreement of the seller.

residue The surplus of an estate after all creditors have been paid.

resolution The formal expression of the will of a meeting. A proposal, proposition or motion that has been duly passed or approved by the required majority becomes a resolution.

respondentia A loan raised on the security of a ship's

cargo on the personal responsibility of the ship's master.

restrictive practices Labour practices designed to preserve particular forms of work for members of certain trade unions.

restrictive trade practices Business practices, often involving open or hidden collusion between suppliers, designed to limit competition and prevent the entry of new firms to a market.

retail The sale of goods or services to the final customer in quantities suitable to the customer's own use.

retailer One who sells retail.

retained income statement (USA) The equivalent of UK *profit and loss appropriation account*.

retained profit Profit that is not distributed to shareholders, partners or owners, but kept back in the organization.

retainer 1. A fee paid to a person in return for the right to call upon that person's services in accordance with agreed terms and conditions. 2. A fee paid to a lawyer to conduct or defend a case.

retention money A part of the contract price which is held back for an agreed period after completion of the contract to allow the customer time to ensure that it has been carried out correctly.

retire a bill To pay a bill on maturity or on its being discounted.

revenue The current income of an organization during a stated period.

revenue account The business account which shows the income and the expenditure charged against this revenue.

reversion The right to property after the death of a person at present in possession or on some other specified event.

revocable letter of credit A *documentary letter of credit* arrangement that can be cancelled or changed by the decision of a foreign buyer without prior notice to the exporter. As such it has little use in foreign trade because it is unlikely to be acceptable to a bank.

revolving credit A type of *documentary credit* which is renewed and available for a series of payments.

rider 1. An addition to a document after its completion. 2. An additional clause to a resolution or verdict.

rig To force up the price artificially in a market by buying and leading others to buy with the object of selling at a profit before others realize that the price has no justification in real value.

right of survivorship The right of joint tenants holding property to enjoy the continuation of such right as long as any of the joint tenants survive.

rights issue An issue of new shares made in the first place to existing shareholders. It takes the form of giving shareholders the right to buy, at a specified price, a stated number of new shares for every so many existing shares already held, e.g. one new for every five shares presently held. The price is usually below the ruling market price of existing shares so that shareholders who do not wish to exercise their rights may sell them in the exchange.

ring A combination of people to secure property at a price far below its market value and to share in the profits.

risk An insurance term used to indicate the life, property, liability, interest or contingency for which insurance cover is being sought or which is covered by a policy.

Ro/Ro Roll on-roll off. A term applied to transport where the goods remain on the vehicle during sea transit.

role playing A training method which requires the participants to adopt and act given parts in an exercise which simulates a real life problem.

royalty A payment to the owner of a property right by a person using that property. The term is used chiefly for the following payments. 1. To owners of mineral rights. 2. To patent holders. 3. To writers and other copyright holders.

rpm 1. Revolutions per minute. 2. Resale price maintenance. See *resale price maintenance*.

run on a bank, building society or other deposit holder A sudden surge in demand for the repayment of deposited money caused by fear that the institution is financially unstable.

running costs or expenses The costs of actually operating a business or piece of equipment as opposed to the *capital cost* of purchasing or replacing the business or equipment.

running days A chartering term for consecutive days, including Sundays and not, therefore, limited to working days.

S

SAE Stamped addressed envelope.

sale and lease-back The sale by a business organization of freehold land or property to a financial institution from which the organization 'leases back' the land or property and continues to occupy and use it. The intention is usually to release some of the capital value of assets for active employment in the business. See *lease-back*.

sale or return When goods are obtained 'on sale or return' it is understood that if they are not used or re-sold within an agreed time they can be returned to the supplier who will refund their cash value less any agreed charge.

sale warrant A warrant issued with a *weight note* when goods are sold for payment by a deposit at the time of sale and the balance by a *prompt date*, to be exchanged for the actual warrant for the goods as soon as the balance of the purchase money has been paid.

salvage 1. Property saved from fire or other disaster. 2. Money payable to those who assist in saving a ship or goods from disaster at sea.

sample A small portion drawn from the main part of goods to test or represent the whole. Commodities such as tea whose quality may vary from crop to crop are generally sold by sample rather than by grade or description.

sampling orders Orders issued by those whose goods are in docks or warehouses, authorizing the wharfinger or warehouse keeper to permit samples to be taken away.

sans recours Without recourse (to me), i.e. 'I accept no liability if this document is not honoured'. This is a phrase that may be added to a bill of exchange by an endorser who does not wish to have any responsibility if the acceptor fails to meet the obligation to pay.

SAYE Save as you earn. A savings scheme involving regular payments which can often be made by deduction from earnings.

schedule A list or inventory.

SCP Simplified Customs procedure. A simplified export procedure available to regular exporters of goods not liable to duty or restriction.

scrip Formerly the term for the provisional certificate of a person's holding of debentures, it is now widely used to refer to any stock or share certificates.

scrip issue A capitalization of reserves by issuing fully paid-up shares free to existing shareholders in proportion to the number of shares currently held.

SDRs Special drawing rights. An international reserve currency created and administered by the International Monetary Fund.

seal Originally an impression in wax made by an

engraved stamp. It is still technically necessary for deeds to be sealed but this is usually achieved by sticking on a small circle of paper (usually red). Even this practice is not always followed for many day-to-day agreements made by individuals whose signatures are unlikely to be disputed. Companies, however, must have a seal as the company is an individual which cannot sign its own name.

search 1. an examination by Customs officers of a ship's cargo. 2. An examination of a register of official records to seek information, e.g. concerning charges or claims to property or to check the history of an individual or company. 3. Any systematic exploration of examination.

searcher A Customs officer charged with the duty of searching.

second mortgage A loan raised on the security of the balance of value of property above the amount of any outstanding claim under the terms of a first mortgage.

second via The second copy of a bill of lading or bill of exchange, sent by different route (or usually by different post) in case the original goes astray.

secondary picket A *picket* mounted by workers at a place other than the place where they are employed. The object may be to block supplies or markets or simply to extend the dispute and put additional pressure on their employer. Secondary picketing may leave the union exposed to the possibility of legal action in the civil courts by the firm subject to the picket.

sector A subdivision of a track on a magnetic computer disk. It represents the smallest portion of data that can be modified by overwriting.

secured creditor A creditor holding security, such as stock certificates or mortgage, sufficient to cover the amount of a debt.

Securities and Exchange Commission The body which protects the interests of investors in United States stock markets.

security Any document giving the holder a right to money, goods or other property not actually in his or her possession. The term is commonly used as a general reference to stocks and shares of all kinds.

seizing The occupation or possession of a freehold estate by one who has the legal right to do so following non-payment of a debt or non-fulfilment of a liability.

sellers over A market term meaning that there are more sellers than buyers.

selling out The sale, by the seller, of securities not taken up by a buyer by the due date stipulated in a sale contract. The buyer is liable for any additional expenses incurred by the seller as a result of the failure to honour the contract.

semiconductor A material such as silicon or germanium, whose electrical conductivity increases with temperature and is intermediate between metals and insulators. Semiconductors of different conductivity can be combined to provide a variety of junctions which are the basis of semiconductor devices.

senior (shop) steward The principal shop steward or one of a group of shop stewards recognized by workers and management as having more authority and wider representational powers than the other stewards and able to negotiate with higher levels of management.

sequestration 1. The placing of any disputed property into the hands of a third person pending settlement of the dispute. 2. Holding the property of another until the profits pay the demands upon it. 3. Taking possession of an estate of a bankrupt in order to distribute it among the creditors.

sequestrator The person entrusted with sequestered property.

set-off A cross-claim arising out of the same matter from which a claim has arisen. The claim is intended to reduce the claim of another without creating a separate action.

settlement 1. The payment of an account or claim. 2. A deed made 'upon consideration of marriage'.

settlement day The last day of the stock exchange settlement.

share The proportion of interest in any undertaking or company. Unless qualified in some way the term 'share', as applied to limited liability company shares, usually means *ordinary share*. A 'share' is really a share in the 'joint stock' of a *joint stock company*. In the USA the term *stock* is normally used for share(s) and *common stock* for UK *ordinary share(s)*.

share capital The amount of shares authorized by the company's *memorandum of association*. See *authorized capital* and *nominal capital*.

shareholders Those who possess shares in a company.

share option scheme See *stock option plan or scheme*.

share register See *register of members*.

shift A division of the 24-hour day into a block of working hours such that one shift of one group of workers may be followed by another with another group. Hence *night shift*, *shift worker*, etc.

ship broker An agent appointed by the owners to transact business relating to ships and to obtain cargo and passengers. The ship broker handles cargo insurance, makes contracts, issues bills of lading and other matters relating to the use of ships.

shipper 1. One who arranges the shipment of goods by sea. 2. (USA) One who transports goods by rail or other means. This wider use is extending to the UK.

shipping bill A Customs document used when

drawback of duty is claimed on goods for re-export or for use on board during transit.

shipping documents The documents needed by the importer to claim goods and complete their entry to the importing country. Under a *documentary collection* they accompany a draft bill of exchange and are released on *acceptance* of the bill or on payment. Under a *documentary credit* arrangement they are presented by the exporter to the bank acting for the importer and if found to be correct an accepted bill is released in exchange. The shipping documents will always include a document of title to the goods such as a bill of lading.

ship's clearance outwards Permission by the Customs for a ship to sail from port.

ship's protest A sworn declaration by the ship's master and crew concerning the circumstances under which the ship or her cargo has been lost or damaged. This may be required by insurance underwriters as a condition of settling a claim.

ship's report A form giving details of ship, crew, cargo and stores carried. This must be handed to the Customs within 24 hours of arrival at any port in the United Kingdom.

shop floor 1. The factory area where manufacturing takes place, where the machines and manual workers are. 2. The workers who work on the shop floor, the manual workers.

short (USA) The equivalent of UK *bear*. Selling short

means selling in the expectation of a price fall. It arises from 'selling short of stock', i.e. selling stock not actually held in the expectation of being able to purchase it at a reduced priced before delivery is required. Hence selling oneself or another 'short' means denigrating the person's value or personal qualities.

short-dated securities Also known as 'shorts', these are loans which have only a short time to run before their maturity date. In the case of government stock the term is applied where the period is less than five years.

shrinkage Unexplained loss of stock, especially in the retail trade, due to causes such as pilferage and error.

SIC Standard industrial classification. A system of classifying sectors of the production system. Continuing efforts are being made to persuade all countries to follow a common system so that realistic international comparisons can be made.

sight bill A bill of exchange payable at sight or on presentation.

sight deposit A bank deposit from which amounts can be paid or withdrawn without prior notice to the bank.

simple bonus A life assurance term for a bonus or profit share declaration which is based on the policy sum alone and not on that sum plus previous bonuses. Contrast *compound bonus*.

simple interest Interest paid to the lender when it becomes due.

simulation A representation of a work process, activity or piece of equipment, and which has certain desired features of the real thing. Simulations are used for training and for work planning and preparation.

sinking fund A fund invested outside the organization and built up from contributions out of revenue. The fund is allowed to accumulate at compound interest until it is required for the renewal of assets or the repayment of debt.

SITC Standard industrial trade classification. A standard adopted under United Nations procedures to classify goods for compulsory trade statistical purposes.

sit-in The action of a group of workers in occupying and refusing to leave their place of work in protest at some action by the employer, often an attempt to delay, prevent or modify the terms of closure or sale of an establishment.

SITPRO Simplification of International Trade Procedures Board, an activity of the British Overseas Trade Board.

sleeping partner A partner who invests money in a partnership but takes no active part in its management. Unless a limited partner under the provisions of the Limited Partnerships Act, a sleeping partner continues to have an unlimited personal liability for the debts of the business.

sliding scale A scale of payments of income rising or falling in set proportions.

slump 1. A severe and continued fall in the level of economic activity. 2. A sudden and severe fall in the level of market demand and hence of market prices for a particular good.

slush fund A fund used for making secret payments in return for favours received or anticipated.

snake A term applied to a currency system operated by a group of countries, such as the European Communities, whereby all the different national currencies of the group are linked together so that a change in the exchange rate of one will affect all the others.

soft currency Currency for which the supply is likely to exceed demand in world currency markets. The exchange value of the currency is, therefore, likely to fall.

software The magnetic tape, disks, or other records of computer programs required to operate a computer.

sole agent An agent who has the sole right to represent a particular principal or to distribute specified products within a defined area.

sole proprietor or **sole trader** A business organization which is owned and controlled by one person.

solvency The state of being able to pay all one's

debts. One who enjoys this enviable state is said to be *solvent*.

sovereign A British gold coin with a nominal value of one pound but whose market value depends on the price of gold.

SP Supra protest. See *protest*.

span of control or **span of management** 1. The actual number of subordinates supervised by a manager. 2. The effective limit to the number of others (subordinates) that a manager can supervise efficiently. This, of course, depends on a wide range of factors.

special crossing A crossing on a cheque specifying the name of the bank into which the cheque is to be paid.

special deposits The additional deposits that commercial banks may have to make with the Bank of England and which are intended to withdraw money from the financial system, when required under a system of monetary control in Great Britain.

special endorsement An endorsement on a bill of exchange or other negotiable document specifying the name of the person to whom the bill, etc., is to be paid.

speciality chain (store) A chain of shops owned and controlled by the same organization and selling the same specialized classes of goods. Contrast *variety chain (store)*.

specie Coined money. Contrast *bullion*.

specification 1. A detailed description or enumeration of something. 2. A detailed description of an invention submitted by an applicant for a patent. 3. A detailed description of a project in building, engineering, etc.

speculation Gambling, especially by dealing in shares, commodities or financial securities.

spin-off effect A consequence, usually a benefit, of a course of action which was not the main reason for undertaking the action. For example, a worker sent on a training course to acquire a special skill may become more conscientious because of the interest shown by the employer. The extra effort is a 'spin-off' from the training course.

spot The price payable now for goods actually available for immediate delivery. The term is used in those markets, e.g. stock and commodity exchanges and the oil market, where securities or goods are also traded on the basis of payment and delivery at some time in the future.

spread 1. The difference or range between two prices, usually between the buying and the selling prices. 2. (USA) The equivalent in a US stock exchange of the British *put* and *call* dealings. See *straddle*.

spreadsheet A computer program which allows figures to be entered on a grid similar to the page of a conventional ledger book. For each position in the grid, a number or formula can be specified

standard shipping note 249

so that altering individual numbers can produce an alternative set of results that use the same basic principles of calculation. This is very useful for modelling and planning.

staff Applied to that part of management that relates to the giving of specialized advice or the performance of specialized services which are not a direct part of the production activity of the organization but which aid its performance, e.g. personnel, accounting, computing services.

stag A stock exchange term for a person who applies for a new issue of shares in the anticipation that the price will rise quickly after the issue so that any shares allocated can be sold at a profit before they have to be paid for.

stale cheque A cheque that remains unpresented beyond the date when a bank will pay it.

stamp duties Government taxes on deeds, stock transfers, conveyances, etc.

standard cost(s) The cost of standard products, produced in standard quantities under standard conditions which may be normal or as required by the conditions of the organization.

standard costing A management technique which makes use of *standard costs*. Observed differences between actual and standard costs are analyzed and their reasons investigated.

standard industrial classification See *SIC*.

standard shipping note An export document

required when a *freight forwarder* or carrier is employed to transport goods. The note is handed to the collecting driver.

standby credit In banking, a *documentary credit* which does not require the presentation of shipping (transport) documents. This credit is very similar to a guarantee.

standing order See *bankers' order*.

standing orders Continuing rules of any organized group or body.

staple Originally a public market to which merchants were obliged to bring their goods for sale, the term has come to be used to denote the principal product or products of a region or country, especially where these have a dominating influence in the regional or national economy.

statement of accounts An account periodically rendered, showing the amounts due by one person or firm to another.

statement of affairs A schedule of assets and liabilities required by statute in cases of bankruptcy or the winding-up of companies.

status enquiry An enquiry to a bank or credit reference agency concerning the creditworthiness of someone with whom business involving credit is contemplated.

statutory declaration Declaration in writing verifying some circumstances or fact and made before a

stock control 251

Commissioner of Oaths, Justice of the Peace, or other responsible person.

statutory meeting The first meeting of shareholders that must, by UK law, be called by a public company within one and three months of the date when it became entitled to commence business.

statutory report The report which, by UK law, must be sent to every shareholder at least fourteen days before the *statutory meeting*.

statutory payments Payments which have to be made in the UK to conform to the requirements of an Act of Parliament. Usually used in relation to payments made by employers to workers on the happening of certain contingencies, e.g. sickness or redundancy.

stet Let it stand. Used to cancel a correction on written, printed or typed matter but in less frequent use since the development of correcting fluids.

stock 1. A general term applying to the transferable securities issued by government, local authorities and companies, especially in the USA. 2. Used to apply to interest bearing securities of government, local authorities and companies in contrast to shares, e.g. Treasury stock, debenture stock, loan stock, etc. 3. An accumulation of goods awaiting processing, use or sale.

stock control A management system for the careful monitoring of the purchase and storage of materials in order to operate at minimum cost consistent with maintaining uninterrupted production.

stock option plan or scheme An arrangement, approved by shareholders, whereby directors and or senior managerial employees may receive shares on preferential terms as a reward for their services.

stock exchange An organized market in which stocks and shares are traded.

stockbroker A stock exchange dealer who acts as a buying or selling agent on behalf of people or organizations outside the exchange.

stockholder One who owns stocks or shares. Also the US equivalent of shareholder.

stock-in-trade All the goods, including materials, work-in-progress, finished product, tools and equipment used to carry on a business activity.

stock-taking A periodic enumeration, check and valuation of all the physical assets held by an organization.

stop An order by a cheque account holder to a bank not to pay a cheque when it is presented. Cheques used with a bank card cannot be stopped.

stop order An instruction to a stockbroker to sell *at best* specified shares if their market price falls to a stated level.

stoppage in transitu The stoppage of goods during their transit from one place to another. The seller has the right to stop transit and prevent delivery of goods if the buyer becomes bankrupt or insolvent between the time of agreement to purchase and payment.

storage location also **store location** Within a computer store the basic unit capable of holding a single item of data.

straddle (USA) The equivalent of a *put and call* arrangement in which a stock exchange speculator has the right to sell stock at a specified price and to buy the same or different stock at a specified price within a specified period.

strategy A programme of action and of resource use designed, over a period of time, to achieve stated objectives.

strike A withdrawal of labour by a group of workers.

structural unemployment Unemployment that is believed to result from changes in the pattern and methods of production and from the difficulties faced by workers in adjusting to a changing demand for labour.

Stubbs Gazette A weekly trade paper which gives a diary of creditors' meetings, mortgages and charges by limited companies, extracts from the Registry of Deeds of Arrangement, Registry of County Court Judgments, notices relating to bankruptcies and windings up and other matters of importance to traders dealing on credit terms.

sub-agent An agent employed by an agent to transact

the whole or part of the business entrusted to that agent by a principal.

sub-contract The employment by a contractor of another firm to carry out work which is part of a main contract.

subject to contract A phrase commonly used in relation to the sale of private houses in England and Wales and indicating that a sale has been agreed subject to completion of the legal formalities to conclude the contract. During this period, however, either side may withdraw leaving the other with no right of recovering costs already incurred and this situation has been much criticized. It does not apply in Scotland.

sub-lease A lease by a lessee to another.

sub-let To let as a tenant to another.

subliminal advertising A form of advertising on film or television whereby messages are flashed so rapidly that the watcher is not conscious of seeing them. Nevertheless they are believed to influence the watcher. Advertising codes normally ban the practice.

subpoena A writ issued by a court of law calling upon a person to appear at a day and place assigned, under a penalty for non-appearance or default.

subrogation The legal right of an insurer, having paid compensation for an insured loss, to stand in place of the insured person and use that person's rights and remedies to reduce the loss. For example, a person whose house has been destroyed by fire may have a legal claim against another whose negligence caused the fire and the insurer could pursue this claim. A *subrogation clause* in the policy usually gives the insurer the right to commence proceedings before the actual payment of compensation. A similar right to stand in place of another can arise in certain cases outside insurance.

subscribed capital The amount of capital subscribed or guaranteed by shareholders to a company.

subsidiary company A company of whose ordinary voting shares 51 per cent or more are held by another company which is thus able to exercise control over its operations.

subsidy Financial assistance given by one to another, especially by the State as a transfer from taxation.

sue To bring an action against another in a civil court.

superannuation Pension payable on retirement.

supercargo Officer on a ship charged with the general duty of looking after cargo and all commercial transactions relating to the ship.

supermarket Although attempts have been made to define this class of store in terms of size and goods sold the term is widely used to describe almost any shop that sells groceries and some other goods mainly by self-service methods.

supply side economics Economic policies that concentrate on microeconomic measures to stimulate supply rather than on the techniques of demand management developed by Keynesian economists.

surcharge 1. A charge made by an auditor on an official of central, or especially local government for a payment which that official had no power to make. 2. An additional charge permitted under the terms of a sale agreement but made after the sale has first been agreed or after publication of advertised prices.

surety One bound by a legal document, called a *bond* to: 1. be answerable for the debt of another if it is not paid when due; 2. be responsible for the performance of some duty undertaken by another.

surrender value The amount of money a life assurance office is prepared to pay a policyholder if the policy is surrendered with no further claim on it.

suspense account An account kept of items which, for any reason, cannot be attributed to any of the normal accounts.

suspension of payment Ceasing to pay any debts on becoming insolvent.

sweat-shop A factory where workers work long hours for low wages, often in poor working conditions and in contravention of safety and fire regulations.

sweetener See *douceur*.

SWIFT Society for Worldwide Interbank Financial Telecommunications. A system for providing international traders with same-day money transfers between banks in different countries.

synergy A term much used to justify business mergers denoting that when two organizations combined the new, larger organization was likely to be more effective than the two separate bodies.

symbol chain A voluntary association of retailers and wholesalers distinguished by a distinctive trade symbol. See also *voluntary chain*.

system In computing, a system is any combination of *hardware*, *software*, documentation and manual procedures which are combined to perform a specific function. The contents of a computer room may be called a system, a set of programs which perform a specific application may be called a 'payroll system' and a piece of hardware which processes special text handling software may be called a *word processing* system.

system X The name of British Telecom's digital telecommunications system.

systems analysis Study, often computer assisted, of industrial and commercial procedures and operations with the object of improving efficiency.

systems analyst The person who carries out systems analysis and who is often responsible for producing a design which is used as the basis for the necessary programming.

T

TAC Type approval certificate. A certificate required before first registration in the UK for certain goods carrying vehicles made in the European Communities.

tachograph An instrument recording a vehicle's movements, required by law in the European Communities for most goods carrying vehicles of over three and a half tonnes gross weight and for most passenger carrying vehicles built to carry more than 9 persons.

take-over The action of one company in acquiring 51 per cent or more of the voting, ordinary shares of another and so gaining the ability to control its activities. In the case of public companies in the UK there is a code of practice which protects the interests of the remaining *minority* shareholders when control has passed in this way.

take-over bid An attempt by a company to gain a controlling interest in another.

talisman Transfer accounting, lodging for investors and stock management for jobbers. The computerized settlement system of the British Stock Exchange.

talon A certificate attached to a transferable bond which can be exchanged for further coupons if all the existing ones have been paid.

tangible assets The term is usually applied to *fixed assets* and refers to actual physical land, buildings, plant and machinery, etc., which is held by the organization. Contrast with investments and other *intangible assets* such as goodwill or trade reputation.

tap stock An issue of British government securities which, in the first instance, is chiefly taken up by the Bank of England to hold until it decides to 'turn on the tap' by releasing the stock at a price which the financial institutions will find attractive. These stocks provide a mechanism whereby the Bank of England can influence the level of interest rates.

tare The weight of the case or container containing goods or the weight of the vehicle, without petrol or other equipment, used for carrying goods. If the tare weight is known the net weight of goods can be found by weighing the loaded vehicle or filled container. Equivalent to US *dead weight*.

tariff 1. A table of charges. 2. Charges or duties applied to goods as they cross national frontiers, usually when being imported to a country.

tasting order An order chiefly used in the wine and spirit trade authorizing the dock company to allow the bearer to taste certain wines or spirits named in the order.

T-bond (USA) Treasury bond, as in Chicago Board of Trade T-bond contract, a contract used for speculative and hedging deals.

telegraphic transfer (express international money transfer) The transfer of money between countries by the use of coded inter-bank telex.

teleprinter A device similar to a typewriter but provided with a signal interface for sending and receiving messages. Teleprinters are tending to be replaced by visual display units.

teletex An improved, higher quality telex service.

teletext A term for the transmission of pages of text and drawings alongside normal television programmes. Examples in the UK are Ceefax (BBC) and Oracle (ITV).

telex A system of communication using teleprinters and the normal telephone channels.

teller A bank cashier who receives and pays out money at a bank counter.

tenant One who holds property, houses or land under another by payment of rent.

tenants in common Two or more people who hold property in undivided shares, the revenue from the property being shared jointly. On the death of one tenant the interest in the property passes to his or her personal representatives. Contrast *joint tenants*.

tender 1. A written offer to supply certain commodities or undertake certain work on specified terms. 2. An offer to purchase securities at a stated price. 3. An offer of money in payment of a debt.

tender-to-contract cover A form of insurance cover provided by the *ECGD* under which exporters are protected against the risk of loss through currency exchange movements in the period between tendering for an export order and obtaining the order.

tenement Land or other property held by a tenant.

tenor The time period at the end of which a bill of exchange reaches maturity, i.e. is due to be paid. See also *usance*.

tenure The manner of holding lands or houses, e.g. freehold or leasehold.

term days The days on which rents fall due. See *quarter days*. Also the days on which the legal 'terms' begin.

terminal A computer terminal is a data input/output device connected to a controlling *processor* to which it is usually subservient and remote.

terminal markets Markets on which *futures* trading takes place, i.e. trading involving periods of time.

test marketing The restricted launch of a new product in a particular area or areas for a certain period of time with the object of learning whether the product is likely to achieve a desired sales level if put into full production and distribution and to see whether any modifications in design, packaging, etc., are desirable before going into large scale production.

T-form A Community transit form required by

Customs when full container or vehicle loads are being transported across European Community frontiers.

third-party Someone not directly connected with another but nevertheless affected by that other person's action. For example a pedestrian struck and injured by a passing motor vehicle.

third-party insurance Insurance protection which provides compensation for legal claims arising out of injury to third-parties or damage to their property.

Thirty-share index The index of prices on the British Stock Exchange which is based on the share price movements of 30 leading British companies. The index is maintained by the *Financial Times*.

ticket day See *name day*.

time and motion study The systematic study of work practices in order to discover the most efficient methods of doing particular jobs or as an aid to management in the negotiation of wage payments, especially when these contain some element of *payment by results*.

time series analysis A statistical technique of analyzing data built up over a period of time in order to identify trends or cycles and to discover the main influences bringing about changes in the data.

time share A term usually applied to a form of collective ownership of property whereby the individual owners each have the right to exercise their ownership rights for a stated period each year. In effect, a person may thus 'buy' a holiday villa for, say, the month of June each year and either occupy it or let it to others for that month.

times covered A reference to the extent to which a company's dividend payment is 'covered' by the profit available for distribution. The number of 'times covered' is found by dividing the amount available for distribution by the amount actually distributed. If the result is less than 1. (unity) then the dividend payment is 'uncovered' or 'not covered'.

tip 1. Information given to a speculator offering advice on a profitable opportunity. 2. A gratuity for service received.

TIR Transport internationale routiers. A permit for sealed vehicles or containers which have previously been inspected by Customs to pass across European Community frontiers with the minimum of further checks, etc.

toll A charge made for the use of a road, bridge, tunnel, river crossing, etc.

tontine A financial plan in which a number of persons pay a certain sum of money for which each is granted an annuity for life. As each member dies his or her share is divided among the survivors until the last survivor inherits the whole.

tort A legal term signifying a wrong which gives rise to an action at law independently of contract.

trade association An association of firms operating in the same commercial or industrial sector. The association seeks to promote the common interests of the firms and to provide specialized services and facilities which will be of benefit to them.

trade bill A bill accepted by a trader or merchant and not by a bank. Contrast *bank bill (1)*

trade discount A special allowance made by sellers to people in the trade.

trade mark A trade mark is some name, description or device stamped or placed on articles by manufacturers or suppliers to distinguish their goods from others.

trade rights The term is used to designate those proprietary rights which, apart from brands and trade marks, belong exclusively to the person or firm owning an established trade or business, e.g. a trade name which, if used by another would mislead the public and divert business.

trade union A worker organization whose object is to promote the interests and improve the working conditions of a particular group or groups of workers.

traded options Options (to buy or sell at stated prices within an agreed period) which can be bought and sold during the option period and exercised by the holder at the end of that time.

trade-off A concession made by one party in return for a concession or benefit granted by another.

trading account One of the business final accounts showing the gross profit or loss resulting from a period of trading.

trading certificate The certificate issued by the Registrar of Companies authorizing a company to commence business.

trading stamps Stamps issued by retailers to customers for accumulation and later conversion to cash or use to purchase other goods.

tramp ship A vessel which does not sail to any fixed schedule but is available to carry cargo as and where required.

transfer A stock exchange form which, when completed and signed, authorizes the company to remove the seller's name from the share register and substitute the name of the buyer.

transfer price The price at which materials, components or products are traded between two parts of the same organization, often two companies situated in different countries but belonging to the same company group. It is often necessary to establish such a price for the purpose of establishing separate profit and loss accounts or to satisfy national Customs, taxation or revenue requirements.

tranship To move goods from one ship to another either directly or after landing.

transhipment bond note A document passed to Customs in relation to goods transhipped while they are under bond.

transit credit A credit issued by a bank in one country, advised or confirmed by another bank in another country to a beneficiary in yet another country, sometimes through a third bank in that beneficiary's country.

transport documents The documents showing that goods have been dispatched from one place to another and which are required under a documentary credit. This is a more accurate term, given the nature of modern transport, than the one still often used, 'shipping documents'.

travellers' cheques Cheques purchased in the home country and cashable at banks, hotels and business firms in most countries of the world.

treasury bills Bills which really take the form of promissory notes, issued by the British Government in return for loans from the Money market. Each week the Bank of England invites tenders for the bills from the financial institutions operating in the market. They are an important form of short-term borrowing for the Government and they provide a useful supply of first class liquid assets for the Money market.

Trinity House An establishment that superintends the interests of British navigation. It is concerned with erecting beacons and lighthouses, with appointing pilots and conducting the examinations of mariners and generally is a major influence on a wide range of marine interests.

trust 1. Money or property held for the benefit of

others by specially appointed persons (often financial institutions) called *trustees*. Such property is said to be 'held in trust'. 2. a large combination of business concerns formed usually with the object of controlling a market (especially USA).

trustee A person appointed by deed, will or law to dispose of or manage the property of another.

trustee status Ordinary shares which can be used as investments by trustees under British law. To qualify, the shares must be of companies registered in the UK, have a paid up share capital of not less than £1 million, and have paid a dividend for at least the previous five years.

trustees in bankruptcy Those appointed by the Court to take charge of and manage a bankrupt's estate during the liquidation of his or her affairs.

TUC Trades Union Congress. The body which represents most of the trade unions in the United Kingdom. It has permanent officials but most members are representatives of affiliated unions. It has leadership and advisory functions and helps to settle disputes between members. It represents the trade union movement as a whole in dealings with employers, the government and the public.

turn The difference between the buying and selling price if this has produced a profit, especially in reference to *jobbers* on a stock exchange.

turnover The total sales revenue before any deduction of expenses, achieved by a business organization during a specified time period.

TWI Training within industry.

type A standard sample, representing a certain quality or crop, used as a basis for an agreement to sell while still in production. The quality of the final crop is guaranteed equal to the quality of the 'type'. If in the event the quality is inferior an allowance is negotiated and any dispute settled by arbitration.

U

uberrima fides See *utmost good faith*, the English equivalent of this Latin legal phrase.

ullage Loss due to evaporation or leakage and not covered by insurance.

ULS Unsecured loan stock.

ultra vires Beyond the powers (of a body). The term is applied to actions of bodies corporate which are beyond the powers granted to them by the documents on which their legal existence depends, e.g. the memorandum of association of a registered joint stock company.

umpire A third person appointed to decide an arbitration case in the event of the arbitrators failing to agree.

under bond Imported goods which are stored in a *bonded warehouse*.

under-capitalized A firm that does not have sufficient financial resources to enable it to support the level of trading it is attempting. The probable result is inability to meet debts as they become due and, unless rescued or provided with further capital, insolvency.

underwriter 1. An official of an insurance office who decides whether or not to insure a risk or the terms under which insurance cover is to be provided. 2.

A member of Lloyd's, also known as a 'name' who, as one of a syndicate of members, accepts full personal liability for an agreed share of all insurances arranged for the syndicate by its underwriting agent. 3. The common term used to refer to the syndicate underwriting agents who actually transact insurance business in the 'underwriting room' at Lloyd's. 4. A financial institution which, in return for a consideration, agrees to purchase the whole or part of any quantity of a new public issue of stock that remains unsold to the public when the offer closes.

undischarged bankrupt A bankrupt to whom a formal certificate of discharge has not been granted.

unearned income Income derived from invested wealth or property as opposed to earnings from work. Contrast *earned income*.

unfair dismissal Dismissal which, in the UK, is deemed unfair as defined by employment protection legislation.

unit trust A form of investment based on a fund, supervised by trustees (usually banks or other reputable institutions) and managed by professional investment managers. The fund is divided into units so that each unit represents a fraction of all the investments of the fund. The units are then sold to the public who may if they wish sell them back to the managers at some future date. Unit holders receive dividends in much the same way as shareholders.

unitary tax A State tax applied in a number of the

United States of America. The tax is based on the world wide operations of certain multinational companies and can result in the double taxation of some earnings.

unladen weight The weight of a vehicle without its load.

unlimited company A company at least one of whose members accepts unlimited liability for the company's debts.

unofficial dispute or strike A labour dispute that has not been accepted as *official* by the trade union(s) whose members are in dispute. The members in dispute are not, therefore, entitled to the support, including financial support, of the union(s) involved.

unlisted security A security that has not been accepted for the stock exchange official list. Although most are likely to be shares in unlisted companies there are some companies whose ordinary shares are on the official list but whose loan stocks are 'unlisted'. The reverse is also possible.

unsocial hours A term applied to work performed at times outside the hours of a 'normal' working day.

up-front Commercial jargon meaning a payment made or required at the time of order, delivery or transfer, i.e. at an early stage in a transaction.

usance The period allowed for payment of a bill of exchange. See also *tenor*.

user-friendly A term applied to a computer software package which gives the user clear, simple and step by step instructions and which does not assume specialized knowledge of computer operations.

USM Unlisted Securities Market. That section of the London Stock Exchange which provides a market for public company stock which is not on the full stock exchange official list but which has been accepted for trading on this smaller exchange. It is becoming normal for new public companies, on conversion from private company status, to seek admission to the USM as a first step towards full acceptance to the official list.

utmost good faith A legal principle applying to certain contracts, notably insurance and partnerships, in which the parties have a duty to disclose all facts material to the agreement whether or not they have been asked specific questions on the matter.

V

value received A term used on bills of exchange when the drawee has received either money or goods from the drawer of the bill which is known as a 'bill for value'.

variable costs Costs which change directly as the quantity of production changes, e.g. the cost of materials used in production.

variety chain (store) A chain of similarly styled retail shops all owned by the same organization and each selling a wide range of different goods, often by a mixture of counter 'cash and wrap' and self-service methods. Contrast *speciality chain (store)*.

VAT Value added tax. A tax levied at each stage of the production process and based on the difference between a firm's sales revenue and the cost of purchased goods and services. The widely used French equivalent of 'VAT' is 'TVA' (taxe à la valeur ajoutée).

VDU Visual display unit. See *visual display unit*.

vendor The seller.

vendue (USA) A public auction.

venture capital Money made available through loans or shares to new and largely untested business enterprises.

verification The process of checking the accuracy of transcription of information from one communication method to another.

vertical integration or **vertical combination** A merger or take-over which involves two firms in the same industry but at different stages of the chain of production. The 'vertical' movement may be 'forward' as when a manufacturer takes over a distributor, or 'backward' as when a manufacturer takes over a producer of basic materials. See also *horizontal combination*.

vicarious liability Liability attaching to one person but arising from the actions of another while acting on behalf of that person, e.g. an employer's responsibility for actions of an authorized employee.

video conference Two or multi-way audio and television links between individuals or groups of people. These may make use of satellite communication.

videotex This is the same as *viewdata*.

video disk A device for storing data, including computer programs, and television pictures.

viewdata The generic term for interactive (two way) systems for transmitting text or graphics stored in computer databases, via the telephone network, for display on a television screen. Prestel is an example.

visibles Physical goods. The term is usually applied to imports and exports. Contrast *invisibles*.

visual display unit An output device that can display both graphic and alphanumeric information. It uses similar techniques to those employed to produce television pictures. It is similar to a *monitor* but is usually associated with a keyboard and used as a terminal to a computer.

voluntary chain An association of retailers and wholesalers designed to gain some of the benefits of large scale operation while retaining their individual independence.

voucher Any document or writing in proof of the payment or receipt of money or of other monetary transactions.

W

wages council A statutory body for the establishment of minimum wages and working conditions in certain occupations where trade union bargaining power is considered to be weak. The councils contain representatives of workers and employers and independent members.

waive Not to pursue a legal right. If, say, payment is waived, the person entitled to receive payment has indicated that no payment is desired.

Wall Street A common term used to refer to the New York Stock Exchange and, more generally, to the New York capital and finance market.

warrant 1. A promise or guaranteed undertaking as in the case of the warrant sometimes issued by companies to holders of a certain type of stock giving them the right to subscribe for future issues of the same or other security. 2. A receipt issued for goods deposited in a warehouse and which is a transferable document of title to those goods.

warranty 1. An undertaking that certain statements are true as in the case of an insurance warranty that the questions on a proposal form for insurance have been correctly answered by the applicant or proposer for insurance. 2. A guarantee, as in *warranted sound* a phrase used when horses are sold at auction.

wasting asset An asset whose value declines as it used up in the production process.

waybill A document containing a list of passengers or goods being carried.

weight note A document issued by a dock authority giving details, including the weight, of a consignment of goods unloaded from a ship.

wharf A landing place for loading or unloading goods on a vessel. Also sometimes used, especially for coal, in relation to a railway.

wharfage A charge for receiving and removing goods on a wharf. The ability to transfer containers direct from ship to road or rail vehicle has, of course, transformed many traditional port practices and charges.

white collar worker An office or other non-manual worker.

wholesale 1. The trade that is carried on between firms at any stage of the production process. 2. Buying and selling in quantities larger than is usual in retail selling to the final consumer. Some wholesale traders may be prepared to sell to the final consumer provided that purchases are made in large quantities.

wild-cat strike A sudden stoppage of work without any serious attempt to settle a grievance by negotiation.

winding-up The closing of business transactions either voluntarily or on order of the Court.

window A rectangular area on a computer display screen inside which part of an image or file is displayed. The window can be any size up to that of the screen and more than one window can be displayed at once.

window-dressing The temporary arrangement of assets and liabilities so that they conform to official requirements at a particular time but give little indication of the real financial situation of the organizations concerned. The term is often used of banks.

without prejudice A term used in correspondence or in making offers and which renders such correspondence or offers incapable of being used in evidence.

without recourse A term sometimes put upon bills of exchange and similar documents when they are sold to another. It means that the buyer has no claim for recovery whatever upon the seller for recovery of a loss should the documents not be paid when due or that the holder of a bill has no claim against an endorser who has added these words after the endorsement, in the event of the bill being unpaid.

word processor A combination of computer and printer. Text is fed into the computer, usually from a typewriter style keyboard, arranged in the form desired and printed. Text may be stored in the computer's memory system and the manipulative powers of the computer used to select, combine, alter or otherwise process the material as required. Clustered word processing systems permit several operators to share printing and filing resources.

work study The systematic study of working practices and procedures designed to increase the efficiency of the process.

work to rule A form of industrial action in which workers stick to the letter of their instructions and interpret them in such a way as to delay work and add to the employer's costs.

worker control A term applied to a business organization where workers and their representatives are in control and entitled to the profits of the enterprise for which they hire capital. This is in contrast to the 'normal' situation where the owners of capital are in control and entitled to profits and who hire labour.

worker co-operative A production organization which is owned and controlled by the workers who work in it. Representatives of the workers are responsible for hiring capital and specialist management skill.

worker participation A management system where worker representatives are invited to discuss problems and take a limited part in the decision-making process. The organization remains under the final control of the directors representing the equity stockholders.

work-in-progress Uncompleted work at any stage of the production process.

working capital The value of current assets less current liabilities. It is a measure of the firm's ability to meet claims for payment.

working capital ratio The proportion that current assets bear to current liabilities.

works council A formal group of management and worker representatives which meets to discuss and seek solutions for common problems.

World Bank The name commonly used to denote the International Bank for Reconstruction and Development, the leading member of the 'World Bank Group' of financial institutions. These are mostly involved in various aspects of promoting and financing the economic development of the less developed countries.

writ A written command or formal order made by a court of law.

write off 1. To close an account by transferring the balance to the Profit and Loss Account. 2. To give a zero value to physical assets, e.g. equipment or stock, in the books of the firm. 3. To damage a vehicle to the extent that the cost of repairs exceed its market value so that it can no longer be regarded as a usable vehicle.

wrongful dismissal Dismissal which is in breach of the employment contract.

X, Y, Z

XD Ex dividend. Stocks are usually purchased together with any rights to dividend or interest accumulated since the last payment. Shortly before the dividend or interest payment becomes due the stock goes 'ex dividend' and payment is made to the registered holder on that date. Purchasers between this date and the payment date have no rights to any accumulated payment. The term is freely applied to share dividend and loan stock interest, to company and to government stock.

yield The annual return on an investment expressed as a percentage of either the cost or the current market value of the investment. Unless specifically stated otherwise the yield quoted in the financial pages of journals such as *The Times* and The *Financial Times* is based on current market price and the last dividend paid, it being assumed that the next dividend will be the same as the last.

yield to redemption The annual or 'flat yield' of fixed interest stock plus or minus the difference between current and maturity value of the stock divided by the length of time to go until maturity.

YTS Youth training scheme.

zero-based budgeting A management budgeting system in which programmes are divided into 'packages' consisting of goals, activities and necessary resources. The budgeted costs are worked out for each package from the ground up.

zero-rate (of VAT) If a firm is zero-rated for purposes of VAT it does not pay any tax on its own value added but it is able to recover the VAT paid on goods and services purchased from other firms. It is, therefore, in a much more favoured position than a 'VAT exempt' firm which does not pay VAT but which cannot recover any tax paid on its production inputs.